WHALE PRIMER

With special attention to the California Gray Whale

By Theodore J. Walker

Produced in cooperation with
the National Park Service

Published by the Cabrillo
Historical Association
P.O. Box 6670
San Diego, CA 92106
(619) 293-5450

First Printing 1962
Second Printing 1965
Third Printing 1967
Fourth Printing 1969
Fifth Printing 1972
Sixth Printing (Revised) 1975
Revised Edition 1979
Eighth Printing 1985

Copyright© Cabrillo Historical
Association 1979

ISBN 0-941032-00-0

Library of Congress
catalog card number 85-062818

Credits

Howard Hall; cover and pages 31, 32
John Dawson; 5–6, 25–26, 37–38
Sea World; title page and pages iv, 8, 12, 13, 14, 15, 21, 43
Dr. T.J. Walker; pages 10, 28, 34
San Diego Zoo; page 35
Golden Gate National Recreation Area; pages 45, 47, 49
Steven Swartz; Technical Adviser
McQuiston & Daughter, Inc.; Design

CABRILLO HISTORICAL ASSOCIATION

The Cabrillo Historical Association is a nonprofit organization which operates under authorization of the federal government and in cooperation with the National Park Service. Its purpose is to provide support for the interpretative and visitor-related services of the Cabrillo National Monument in San Diego, California.

The Association's activities include the publication of books and leaflets about the Monument and its interpretative themes, sponsorship of seminars, foreign language brochures, slide presentations, cooperation with the Cabrillo Festival, and related activities. The Association also provides visitor services for the sight and hearing impaired and disabled visitors, and helps with the development and maintenance of the library and certain equipment at the Monument.

In addition to *The Whale Primer,* the Cabrillo Historical Association publishes a general guide to the Monument by Joseph E. Brown, *The Cabrillo National Monument; The Old Point Loma Lighthouse* by F. Ross Holland; *Cabrillo's Log 1542-1943, A Voyage of Discovery* summarized by Juan Paez; and annual publication of the papers from the Cabrillo Festival Historic Seminars.

FOREWORD

The annual migration of gray whales from their summer feeding areas in the Arctic seas to their calving areas in the lagoons of Lower California brings them close to the headlands of Point Loma on which is located the Cabrillo National Monument. Although this monument boasts one of the great panoramic views of the world it is the passage of the gray whales from December to March which attracts the great number of visitors during this period.

It was, therefore, logical for the Cabrillo Historical Association to publish an aid for the many whale watchers who came to the monument. No one was more qualified to undertake this task than Dr. T. J. Walker the founder of the whale observatory at Cabrillo National Monument. This was the first such observatory on the West Coast. After receiving his Ph.D. in 1948 Dr. Walker joined the National Park Service as a ranger-naturalist. He later became associated with Scripps Institution of Oceanography as a research marine biologist specializing in sensory orientations in fish. Dr. Walker is widely recognized as a scientist and an authority on the gray whale.

For the second time within a four year period the format of this publication has been changed to increase its value to the reader. The text has been updated and new illustrations added. For their assistance in this project appreciation is sincerely expressed to the several organizations who have made illustrations and material available. Credit is given where appropriate. The Committee is most appreciative of the cooperation extended by the staff of Cabrillo National Monument and particularly by Superintendent Thomas Tucker and Terry DiMattio.

Carl F. Reupsch, Chairman
Lester Earnest
Frederick Trull
Richard B. Yale
Publication Committee, Cabrillo Historical Association

CONTENTS

INTRODUCTION

The Whale Primer provides a brief introduction to one of nature's most interesting creations, the whale. The principal star of this primer is the California gray whale which in recent years has become a major visitor attraction in southern California. Although there is a tremendous number of technical and popular writings about whales, there is still great mystery about them. Whales spend most of their lives below the surface of the sea. Because of this most of our knowledge comes from studying the bodies of stranded or beached whales and surface observations.

Many of the papers on whales are published in journals of limited distribution. Others are long since out of print and much of the primary historic records can be found by examination of records which exist only in one particular library. In the preparation of this manuscript hundreds of books and over 4,000 papers were catalogued, of which the most important were available and examined. The author was particularly fortunate to have Japanese and Russian friends who gave gladly of their time to insure coverage of these important papers.

The author made an extensive condensation of the facts in order to reduce the overwhelming details that merely obscure the broad picture. It is hoped that you will gain an awareness of the extreme mastery by whales of the marine environment. We have included other basic concepts of biology which are clearly illustrated by the natural history of whales.

Each life form on earth represents millions of years of adaptation and change. Each in its own way is unique and therefore worthy of preservation. All life forms including whales are their own reason for existence. The interdependence of all life forms revealed by ecological investigations provide the strongest arguments not to interfere. Man is but a party to this grand scheme. We hope that you will be stimulated to join forces with those of us who feel that man should preserve those forms of life which add so much interest, beauty and knowledge to man's awareness.

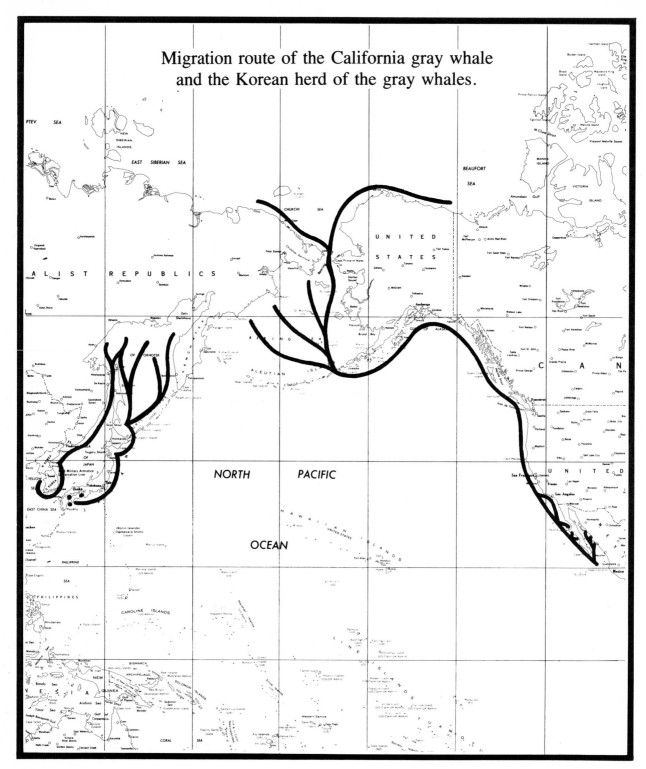

Migration route of the California gray whale
and the Korean herd of the gray whales.

MIGRATION ROUTES

The migration of the California gray whale is one of the most remarkable natural history events in the world today. The majority of these whales journey southward just off the shore of southern California and Baja California, Mexico during January and February. Although a few early migrants may pass San Diego early in December, they are not abundant until Christmas. Whales usually travel north well offshore. Considerable numbers can be found seven miles offshore at the Coronado Islands where they stop apparently to feed.

Only 30 years ago this species was so rare that little hope was held that it could ever recover. Today the species appears out of danger, thanks to international cooperation among the whaling nations which stopped the slaughter of this unique whale. Now it is not at all unusual to see between 50 and 75 whales a day during the peak of the migration.

One of the finest locations for viewing this migration is the Cabrillo National Monument which commands an almost aerial view of the coastline. Here individual whales can be watched for at least an hour as they move into view from the north and at last recede to the south. The observatory is one of the most popular centers for wintertime activities in southern California. There is no other marine animal which can be seen with such certainty in its natural element.

Migrating animals have always fascinated man who considered them harbingers of the seasons. Man continues to puzzle over the mysteries of how these animals are able to navigate so precisely and how they are able to maintain such timetables. Whereas other migrating animals pass broadly through an area, the California gray whales proceed usually near shore and at times just beyond the surf zone. It is hard to realize that 3 months earlier these whales had started from their summer quarters in the Arctic Ocean and the Bering Sea en route to their winter quarters in the lagoons along the western coast of Baja California. Between these two areas lie 4,000 miles of seemingly trackless ocean. With the advent of spring the whales must be on their way back again to their summer grounds. This is the longest known migration in the world undertaken by any mammal.

Although all the large whales make extensive travels, only the gray whale and the right whale spend so much time in sight of land. The other species are truly oceanic at all times, and never seem abundant because of the vastness of the oceans. Like the gray whale they congregate in polar seas during the summer months, moving into temperate and subtropical waters for the winter months.

SEASONAL HABITAT

One cannot help but be impressed with the remarkable utilization of time by the whales whose lives seem to be divided into two principal seasons, a summer feeding period and a winter period of reproduction. Each of these major activities is preceded and followed by a tremendously long migration. Nearly half of every year must be devoted to this activity. The extreme length of the migration leaves little time for the whales to wander aimlessly or carelessly. Whale species which summer in the Antarctic continue to do so as do the same species in the Arctic waters, and only rarely does one pass through the wide belt of equatorial water to venture into the other hemisphere. There is no evidence that the gray whale has ever done so.

Once on the summer grounds the whales occupy themselves with feeding almost continuously during the long polar day. Even though the food may be patchy, the whales seem to find it quickly, spending a minimum of time in search. By the onset of autumn they are fat and all the babies are weaned.

It is uncanny that the various species all manifest the instinctive reaction to vacate the polar regions at the proper time, thus avoiding suffocation by freezing of the sea's surface. Again the seeming miracle of aptness is evident, for the whales swim unerringly out of the

The representative cetaceans, shown here to scale, illustrate the diversity of this mammal order. The cetaceans are divided into two suborders known as Odontoceti and Mysticeti, the toothed whales and the baleen whales, respectively. The toothed whales are numbered 1 through 13 in the identifying legend, while the baleen whales are 14 through 22. The largest toothed whales are the sperm whale (4) and the killer whale (10). Toothed whales also include the dolphins (1,2) and porpoises (4) which are the smallest cetaceans. The baleen whales are generally large, although the pigmy right whale (14) is an exception. The California gray (15) is believed to be primitive in many ways and possibly a descendent of the ancestral type from which modern whales evolved. The other baleen whales are divided into the roquals, (those with dorsal fins and grooved undersides) and the right and bowhead whales (which lack both of these characteristics). Today's whales evolved from ancestors which have been traced back through fossils, some 50 million years. Little is known about their history before this hazy period of time when ancestors of these mammals made their way back to the sea.

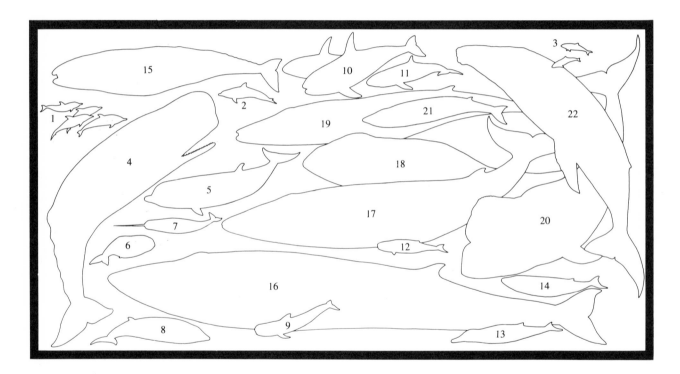

Toothed Whales (Suborder Odontoceti)
1 Common (Atlantic) Dolphin *(Delphinus delphis)*
2 Atlantic bottle-nosed Dolphin *(Tursiops truncatus)*
3 Harbor porpoise *(Phocoena phocoena)*
4 Sperm whale *(Physeter catodon)*
5 Atlantic bottle-nosed whale *(Hyperoodon ampullatus)*
6 White (beluga) whale *(Delphinapterus leucas)*
7 Narwhal *(Monodon monoceros)*
8 Cuviers beaked whale *(Ziphius cavirostris)*
9 Common blackfish (pilot whale) *(Globicephala melaena)*
10 Pacific killer whale *(Grampus rectipinna)*
11 False killer whale *(Pseudorca crassidens)*
12 Pigmy sperm whale *(Kogia breviceps)*
13 True beaked whale *(Mesoplodon mirus)*

Baleen Whales (Suborder Mysticeti)
14 Pigmy right whale *(Caperea marginata)*
15 California gray whale *(Eschrichtius gibbosus)*
16 Blue (Sulphur-bottom) whale *(Balaenoptera musculus)*
17 Fin-back (Fin) whale *(Balaenoptera pysalus)*
18 Bowhead whale *(Balaena mysticetus)*
19 Sei whale *(Balaenoptera borealis)*
20 Atlantic right whale *(Eubalaena glacialis)*
21 Little piked (Minke) whale *(Balaenoptera acutorostrata)*
22 Hump-backed whale *(Megaptera novaeangliae)*

dangerous areas toward warmer and calmer seas. Because of the extremely wide band of winter storms, whales must move below 30° latitude to be clear of the areas of stormy seas. Migration stops as soon as they are sufficiently clear of these. In the adjoining lagoons gray whales undertake the other essential link in the chain of life, reproduction. By spring the babies are strong enough and fat enough to accompany their mothers.

Feeding—Filter Whales

Whales do not feed extensively while migrating. For the most part there is not time enough, nor is the food plentiful enough. However, in the polar seas the whale's food is plentiful enough to discolor the water. On close examination, the discoloration proves to be caused by thousands of tiny shrimp-like creatures which are very slender and except in the Antarctic are usually less than one-half inch in length. These creatures congregate in swarms near the surface to feed on microscopic plants known as diatoms. The whales need only swim back and forth through these cloudlike aggregations to fill their mouths quickly with water and food. With each mouthful, the water is expelled between the jaws through a mat of fibers, known as baleen, or whalebone, which hangs down from the upper jaw. The food, which is retained on the mat, falls down onto the tongue and is swallowed. The work of pushing out several tons of water with each feeding is done by the tremendous tongue.

The fiber mats are the frayed inner side of enormous hornlike plates of baleen which grow down from the palate. The main body of each plate is placed edgewise to the outgoing water so that many plates are required to complete the mat which runs from the tip of the jaw to the corner of the mouth. These plates vary in size and stiffness from species to species. Some of the plates from the mouth of the bowhead whale are 12-14 feet long, whereas those of the finback whale measure 2-4 feet. There may be more than 200 plates per side in the

filtering structure. The frayed inner edge is constantly breaking off and the plates keep growing and fraying to provide the necessary thickness for the mat. The baleen was called whalebone by the whalers, and that term is still used in commerce. The baleen plates are not bones nor could they be mistaken for them. The whalebone was assiduously collected and sold to be made into a variety of objects such as umbrella stays, corset stays, buggy whips and other articles which today are made of steel or plastic. There was a great demand for the product and a bowhead whale produced over a ton and one-half of whalebone valued in the 17th century at over 400 English pounds, equivalent to about $10,000 today.

It has been observed that the coarseness and thickness of the baleen is suited to the size of the food which is filtered. For example, the sei whale, which feeds on minute food, has a filtering surface which resembles fine wool. The blue whale, which feeds on much larger creatures including fish, has the coarsest filter. Generally, fish occur only in the diets of the blue, finback and other rorquals that swim fast enough to engulf them. Here, the fish are weak-swimming, schooling fishes. The gray whale, unlike the other filter feeders, feeds on bottom-dwelling crustaceans known technically as amphipods. These organisms, occurring principally in shallow water, keep the gray whales close to the shores of Siberia and Kamchatka and Northern Alaska.

To prepare for the long fall migration it must have not only ample food, but time in which to collect it. Although the whales may not all be far enough north to have a 24-hour day, there is enough twilight to let them feed the clock around if indeed they locate their food by sight. In order to take advantage of the prodigious amounts of food available, whales have a huge 3-chambered stomach. It is not at all uncommon to find 5 to 10 wheelbarrow loads of food in the stomach. No one yet knows how fast the food passes through the alimentary tract.

The small to minute animals on which the whales thrive are not uniformly concentrated, but occur at special places where oceanographic processes have enriched the surface waters with cold, nutrient-rich, sub-surface water. The principal oceanographic action that enriches the water at the surface is called upwelling,

''To appreciate fully the nature and the biology of whales, one must know that their ancestors were terrestrial mammals.''

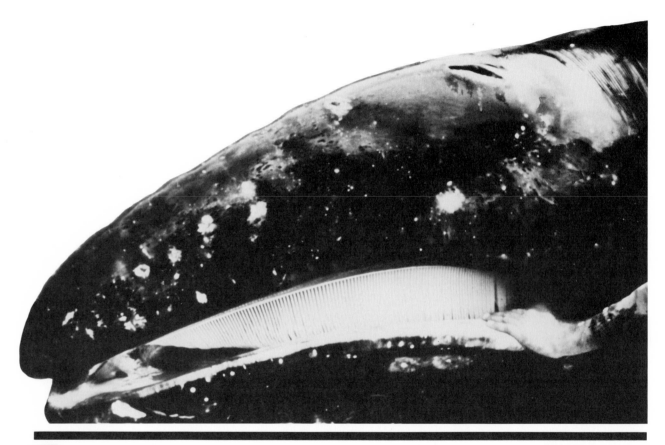

Food filtering is made possible by the mat-like baleen. It consists of rows of flexible, horny plates growing down from each side of the palate. Each of the numerous plates has a fringed inner border and their combined function is that of a sieve. Krill laden water, taken into the mouth is forced through the baleen where the food is trapped for swallowing. Thus, the world's largest animal feeds on some of the smallest.

which can be induced by a number of geophysical conditions. Two chief places where upwelling occurs are along the edge of the polar icecaps and along the junction of strong currents.

Upwelling is one of the ways nature refertilizes the surface waters which are otherwise deficient in nutrients. Whenever the ocean surface is fertilized, the microscopic plants begin to grow and multiply, discoloring the water to a green, brownish, or reddish color. If the subsurface waters continue to be pumped to the surface, the growth continues and a rich pasture results. The animals which begin to crop this are the small shrimp-like animals, and when they have thrived and reproduced, they suffice to nourish the whales.

The other all-important factor in the fertility of the polar seas is the length of day, which provides ample time for the sun's energy to be entrapped by plants. By autumn, the days have shortened and night begins to predominate. At this time the microscopic plants stop growing and form resting stages which protect them through the long winter.

Not all food ingested produces the fatty blubber. Much is used for keeping the animals warm in the bitter cold water (0 to 8 degrees Centigrade or 32-46° F). Pregnant females support the growth of the baby to be, and nursing mothers don't wean the infant whales until late summer when they are 8 months old. Some idea of the nutritional requirements of a growing infant can be obtained from the fact that Gigi, a captive gray whale, consumed 1600 pounds of squid a day by the time she was released at the age of 1¼ year. This whale slept 80% of the time. Whales might be thought of as huge natural tankers carrying enough oil to provide for long periods of fasting. Unlike those mammals which avoid starvation by winter hibernation, the whale is able to migrate away from inhospitable seas into warmer waters where they can then reproduce and care for the new young. The strain on the mother at this time must be considerable for her baby grows at a prodigious rate. It has been calculated that a blue whale baby grows about 10 pounds per hour, gaining a ton every 9 days.

Although there are at least nine species of filtering whales, each seems to largely depend on a different kind of shrimp-like animal, and the different kinds are usually not found together. As a result, the various species of

whales are not in constant competition with each other. Structurally a species may be more suited to feeding on one kind of food: the porosity of the baleen and the shape and size of the head varies from species to species. Right whales have long and wide heads, which permit a large intake of water and the accommodation of a tremendous set of baleen filters. In fact, their heads may constitute nearly one-third of the total body. The whales of the rorqual group are more streamlined and have proportionately smaller heads. To compensate for this limitation, the floor of the mouth is pleated on the outside so that it can balloon out like a huge scoop each time the mouth is filled.

The right whales, incidentally, were so named by the early whalers to designate these species as being suitable for the primitive whaling. The majority of the whales were not hunted because they sank as they died, or were too fast-moving or too wary to be approached and lanced.

EVOLUTION OF WHALES

To appreciate fully the nature and the biology of whales, one must know that their ancestors were terrestrial mammals. It is indeed impossible to account for all the steps which were necessary for this difficult reentry of the oceans. However, the fossil records for whales are numerous and permit at least a partial reconstruction of the evolutionary steps. Whales have not only completely mastered this difficult habitat, but have also diverged to crop a variety of marine foods. Biologists have generally dramatized the earlier conquest of land by marine organisms, but have given less attention to this more recent and perhaps more difficult reentry of the marine world.

Breathing Adaptations

Not only have whales become completely aquatic, but they have been able to eliminate nearly all the design features that fitted them for life on land. Air breathing

Air enters and leaves the whale's respiratory system through one or two blowholes in the head. The two prominent blowholes in this baby gray's head lead directly to the lungs without entering the pharynx. In just a few seconds the whale can exhaust 80 to 90% of its stale air and refill its lungs. (The wrinkled head and clean skin are typical of baby grays.)

remains, and this does not seem to be much of a hardship because of special adaptations. Great improvements in the conservation of oxygen have made really long dives possible. The subtlety of this accomplishment is only partially understood by scientists. Diving mammals are able to shut down those bodily activities that contribute little to the diving mission. These activities can be resumed later when oxygen is available. It is also normal for warm-blooded diving vertebrates to incur an oxygen debt by borrowing from stockpiles present in the tissue fluids and muscles. After a long dive a whale will often idle at the surface in order to completely free the body of the excess carbon dioxide and to pay back the oxygen debt. The greater the debt the longer the surfacing and the greater the number of breaths that must be taken.

When a whale surfaces to breathe the act of exhaling is called ''spouting'' or ''blowing.'' Whenever a whale has been submerged for a normal dive the air in the lungs becomes saturated with moisture from the blood. The exhalation of this spent air is accomplished very quickly by forcing the air out under pressure by the diaphragm, and the sudden expansion of the expelled air produces sufficient cooling to condense the moisture. This cloud or fog is the most conspicuous feature of a surfaced whale, particularly when the spout is 10 to 15 feet high. Within a minute's time the fog is usually scattered and heated enough to disappear. The duration of the spout depends principally on the temperature of the surrounding air, the amount of moisture condensed from the breath, and the local surface wind. At the higher latitudes air temperatures are low enough that the spout may persist for several minutes. It is possible to recognize some of the whale species by the form and size of the spout.

Breathing is accomplished by means of the powerful diaphragm which forces out 85% of the air contained in the lungs in less than one second. Inhalation is achieved in an equally short period when the blowhole is well clear. The breathing act is generally both visible and audible. The release of air produces a very loud ''whoosh'' which can be heard for quite a distance on a quiet day or night. The nostrils are called blowholes. In order to facilitate breathing they have been moved in the course of evolution from the tip of the snout to the top of the head (with the exception of the sperm whale) to

prevent waves from flooding the lungs. During diving, the pressure of the water operates in such a way as to close the nostril from the outside, so that, regardless of depth, there can be no leak. A whale surfaces to breathe moving with sufficient momentum to carry itself ahead and down to a depth at which the flukes can stroke again in both directions to generate full power. Should the whale be floating at the surface, for example when asleep, it will elevate the head for a breath by levering its tail down. The backward momentum and gravity will then submerge the head, the tail will dangle downward, and the head will droop as well. Daytime siestas are punctuated by a head bob every five minutes. This breath is emitted with virtually no mist, making it difficult to spot.

The nostrils communicate directly with the lungs rather than share a portion of the throat as is customary in other air-breathing vertebrates. This means that the whale's mouth and throat can be full of water without danger of flooding the lungs and that it is unnecessary to empty such a spacious cavern prior to breathing. Furthermore, it is unlikely that a whale could keep his mouth closed enough to prevent flooding through the baleen because there is no upper lip over this device.

When the whale dives to its operational depths the water pressure collapses the air sacs of the lung forcing the air back into the supply tubes which are kept from collapsing by support rings. By this means the bend-producing nitrogen can not build up in the blood sufficiently to produce the bends. Although a whale can be sighted by the telltale spout, a frightened whale may elude detection by exhaling just before surfacing, so that nothing more than a foamy patch is produced. Under these situations the whale does not expose the usual amount of buoyant head, but only the nostrils. A disturbed whale can dive, and then surface a mile or two away, or it may not move at all, preferring to hide on the bottom or among rocky reefs or in the kelp.

Swimming Adaptations

The most essential features needed for the successful invasion of the marine habitat were those necessary for efficient propulsion. Fish, eons before, had solved the hydrodynamic challenge necessary for movement through such a resistive medium. The solution required a

''The power developed by muscles in whales is prodigious,
capable of driving a 100-ton body through the water
at speeds up to 20 knots.''

streamlined form with a tail for propulsion, placed at the very end of the body. Extra fins were employed for maneuvering and for balancing. Whales, too, have reached the same solution. As a consequence all whales look more or less alike, differing principally in the degree of streamlining, shape of head, color and size. In a whale's streamlined body there are no sharp discontinuities between the head, the neck, the trunk, and the tail. Instead these features grade imperceptibly one into the other. The only discontinuity is the end of the tail which is expanded into the fanshaped flukes.

These flukes are driven up and down in contrast to the tail fin (caudal fin) of a fish, which is driven sidewise. Whales have along either side of the backbone long banks of muscle, which attach to the tail flukes by tendons. Thus the streamlining of the body is little disturbed in whales, as it is in most fishes by the bending of the hind part of the body from side to side. Some fishes, however, notably the tunas, retain a rigid streamlined body and drive little more than the tail fin back and forth. In both whales and tunas almost the entire muscle mass is devoted to swimming. The power developed by these muscles in whales is prodigious, capable of driving a 100-ton body through the water at speeds up to 20 knots. Wounded whales can smash a 20-foot whaleboat to bits with a single slap of the flukes.

The hind limbs which were useful on land were eliminated in the evolution of whales and all that has persisted are vestigial bones or cartilages buried deep within the surface of the body. The forelimbs underwent reduction and modification into flippers which assist in the turning and diving. The flippers are useful in other ways, providing, for example, a platform on which the baby may stay when danger threatens. They are also useful during courtship and mating, but not for combat. The toothless whales do not have too much to fight with but they may strike an adversary with the powerful tail flukes.

Whales are almost completely hairless, save for a few bristles on their heads (particularly well developed in the gray whale). Certainly the elimination of hair has improved streamlining and has reduced the frictional drag. Furthermore, continuously wet hair could not have been of much value in keeping the whale warm. It is also possible that a hairy whale would have been very much bothered by skin parasites which might well have flourished in the quiet water between the hairs.

If the physical properties of water led whales to assume a common shape through the process of natural selection they did at least, by the buoyant effect, free the animals of the need for structural and muscular developments to support themselves against the pull of gravity. Free of this structural problem, whales were able to evolve into the largest mammal that the world has ever known. As they became larger, they had to shift in their feeding to slower and less maneuverable prey. It would appear that the porpoises, which feed on the rapid-swimming, elusive fishes, have remained small through the ''survival of fittest.'' The sperm whales which have specialized to feed on the jet propelled squid

"Wounded whales can smash a 20-foot whaleboat to bits with a single slap of the flukes."

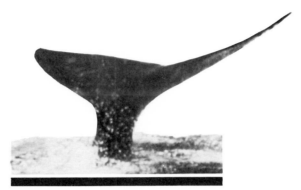

have evolved into much larger whales because they could capture the squid either by stealthy approach or by sucking the squid into the mouth, thus counteracting its jet.

C ETACEAN TYPES

Whales are known technically as cetaceans (pronounced seh-TAY-shuns). This grouping also includes the dolphins, porpoises and close relatives such as narwhal and pygmy whales. Some of these types are briefly introduced here. The known species occurring in North American waters are listed in the Appendix. Size alone is not a criterion of classification: for example, the unrelated pygmy and dwarf sperm whales and the dwarf right whale are much smaller than the killer whale, which is classified in the dolphin family.

Porpoises and Dolphins

The various porpoises and dolphins are mostly eaters of fish. They are certainly the most numerous of all the cetaceans, making up in numbers for their small size (6 to 10 feet), with a few ranging between 20 and 30 feet. Porpoises and generally dolphins congregate around schools of fish. Therefore fishermen are constantly on

the lookout for them. Since not infrequently the porpoises break the surface of the water, leaping completely clear as if to look around, they are not difficult to locate. Porpoises and dolphins can be seen most frequently in coastal waters where fish are most abundant, but some, including those utilized by tuna fisherman, inhabit the high seas. The porpoise and dolphin families contain many species and it is beyond the scope of this treatise to differentiate them all. However, these families include such unique forms as the killer whale, narwhal, white whale (or beluga, as it is known to the Eskimos), and the pilot or black whale. Generally one associates cetaceans with the ocean, so it may come as a surprise to learn that four dolphin species live in such major rivers as the Amazon, La Plata, Ganges, and Yangtze.

The name "dolphin" (not to be confused with the dolphin fish) is generally applied to species of small to moderate size having the mouth protruding beyond the head as a beak or snout, whereas in "porpoises," the front of the head is blunt or gently rounded. It is impossible to avoid confusion if one uses common names to separate the various whales. Even though the word "whale" in a general sense covers all the kinds, to some it connotes the larger species. Such a distinction is wholly arbitrary, and cannot properly differentiate the natural groupings of whales to which zoologists have assigned technical names. It would be impossible to summarize the variety of common names which many of the species have acquired through the centuries. The only

The dolphin, a small, toothed whale, can literally walk on water. Its small size and tremendous propulsive power permit it to remain in this position for a few seconds. Like other whales, most of its musculature is devoted to propulsion with power delivered to the twin flukes. Forelimbs are used mainly for maneuvering. The dolphins speed, agility and learning ability have made it a favorite in marine exhibits.

The narwhal, an arctic inhabitant, is unique among whales for its spiraled tusk. This strange, overgrown tooth is seen only in males. Its function is unknown but, like a man's beard, it may simply be a secondary sex characteristic. It may also be important in the narwhale's social behavior. Its use for feeding is doubtful.

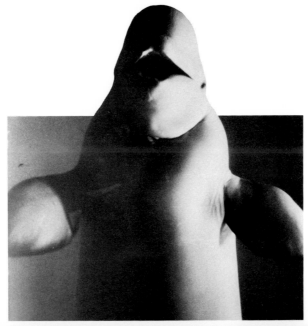

Like the narwhal, the white-skinned beluga prefers the icy waters of the North. They are small, slow-swimming whales, often seen traveling in pods of several hundred individuals. In open water they are easy prey for killer whales, while their curiosity and lack of fear of man has made them equally easy prey for the Eskimo. When in danger, belugas may swim under the ice where they rely on their excellent sonar system for navigating. Like the dolphins and porpoises, belugas have a complex speech. It consists of at least 11 distinct calls, presumably used in communicating within the pod. The larger male beluga grows to about 15 ft. in length and can weigh 1½ tons.

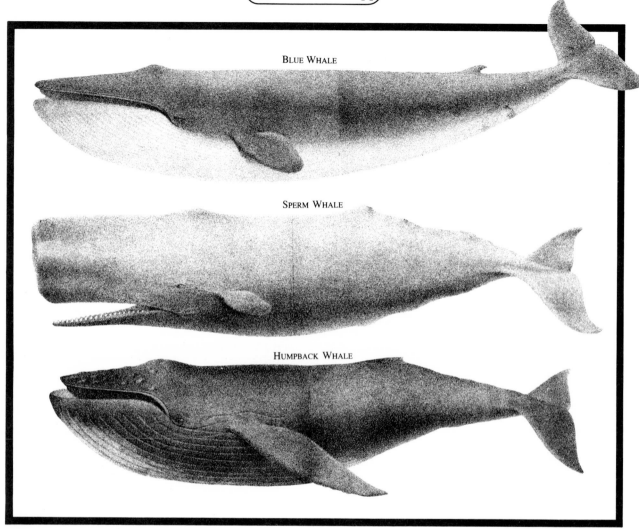

BLUE WHALE

SPERM WHALE

HUMPBACK WHALE

The blue whale, largest animal ever to inhabit the earth, can approach 100 ft. in length and weigh over 140 tons (the record is 142.8 tons, determined by weighing one, piece by piece, in a factory ship). Blues can devour 8 tons of krill a day! Hunted into near extinction, the blues are making a slow come-back under international protection.

The sperm whale (Moby Dick), largest of the toothed whales, grows up to 55 ft. and can exceed 50 tons. At this time they are the most hunted of the whales with about 15,000 slaughtered yearly. A favorite food of the sperm whale is the giant squid.

The humpback whale grows to 50 ft. and can weigh 35 tons. Its huge wing-like flippers and peculiar spinning motion as it breaches make identification easy. The humpback's sluggish movement and great oil yield made it the target of relentless whalers until recently. In 1966 both sperm and blue whales became fully protected.

solution is to refer to the whales by the technical names which connote relationship. (For readers who desire this differentiation, a brief listing of the groups, and representatives of each, are provided in the Appendix.)

Squid Eaters

The bottlenose whales, members of the toothed whale grouping which are nearly toothless, also feed on squid. Porpoises and dolphins, in contrast, possess many sharp conical teeth on both the upper and lower jaws, although the narwhal, which is related to them, breaks the rule by being toothless save for the tusklike canine of the male (either the right or left tooth elongates to produce an 8-foot spear; the other tooth does not break the gum, and in the female both are rudimentary and not externally evident). The bottlenose whales have but a single pair of teeth in the lower jaw (2 pairs in one species), and their relative, the sperm whale, has 18-28 conical teeth per side on the lower jaw, and these when fully grown may be 8 inches long. Pockets are provided in the toothless gum of the upper jaw to accommodate the teeth when the mouth is closed.

The decline in the number of teeth in the sperm and bottlenose whales is thought by some to be the elimination of structures that are no longer useful. Whereas a porpoise's long mouth, bristling with sharp teeth, insures the hooking and retention of a slippery active fish, a small mouth with a few teeth is adequate to crush and slurp down the squid and the weak-swimming fishes of the ocean depths.

The sperm whale is the largest of the squid feeders (the male reaching 60 feet). The diminutive counterparts, the pygmy sperm whale reaches 13 feet and the dwarf sperm whale only 9 feet. These small species are rather rarely encountered whereas the sperm whale has abounded in temperate and warm seas. The beaked whales complete the groups that seem to be specialized for feeding on squid and small pelagic fishes. Besides the modification of the mouth some of these whales are noted for their ability to dive to great depths, where their food abounds. Not only can they dive to great depths, but they can stay submerged for long periods—up to an hour! Sperm whales have been found entangled in the submarine cables which were known to be on the bottom at a depth of 3,000 feet. It is clear that such feeding habits have opened up vast areas of the oceans to these species.

Filter Whales

The whalebone whales seem to have undertaken two different lines of specialization in feeding: The right whales developed an enormous head with very large filter plates, whereas the rorquals have small filter plates and are much more streamlined. The ability of the latter to gather food is increased by the pleated throat. The right whales lack a dorsal fin and are decidedly less streamlined. The rorquals (see p. 6) have a dorsal fin. There are two species which do not exactly fit in either group. The humpback whale appears to be like the rorquals in that it has a pleated throat and a suggestion of a fin. It is however, a very bulky, slow-swimming species. The California gray whale, apparently, is intermediate between the two groups and is commonly thought to be a survivor of the ancestral stock from which both groups may have differentiated. It has only two to four throat grooves and the barest stump of a dorsal fin. The gray whale, like the right whale, has been slow to recover from whaling. It is likely that the populations were never very large. Only the rorquals seem to have the numbers needed for large whaling operations.

SIGNIFICANCE OF BLUBBER

Heat Conservation

As whales extended their operations into the icy waters of polar regions or into the cold waters of the ocean depths, they had to evolve means of keeping warm. Anyone who has attempted to swim in cold water knows how quickly one loses his body heat and becomes chilled. Whales minimize the heat loss by accumulating a thick layer of fat just below the thin surface of the skin. This fatty layer, called blubber, not only keeps the whale warm, but it also provides food storage.

Extensive areas of the whale, however, including the flippers and the large tail flukes are not blanketed with fat. It has been observed that the blood going into these structures gives up its heat not to the outside but to the veins that parallel and surround the arteries. By this anatomical feature most of the heat which would otherwise be lost to the water is recaptured by the veins, which deliver the heat back into the body. Of course, this means that the tissues of the tail flukes and flippers function at temperatures much lower than those within the body. Here we find that nature is using the principal of the heat exchanger, which was evolved long before man discovered it or put it to work in air conditioning.

Heat losses are minimized in the largest whales by the fact that the mass of the whale in which heat may be stored increases approximately as the cube of the length, whereas the heat passing through surface is controlled by surface area, which increases only as the square of the same dimension. This no doubt explains why the new born baby is so large, one-third the length of mother, and why so much of the total growth is achieved in the first year; and also why single births predominate.

Whales are so well insulated that they stay quite warm 24-36 hours after death. Whalers must process the whales quickly, for otherwise, at the elevated body temperature, decomposition proceeds most rapidly and ruins much of the meat. It is possible that the baleen-bearing whales do not cross the warm equatorial waters where they would overheat. No one has yet determined whether the newborn young have a sufficient layer of fat to protect them from the cold water, and it has been suggested that whales calve in temperate waters to prevent the babies from being chilled. However, there are cetaceans, including the narwhal and the white whale, that calve in Arctic waters.

Buoyancy

Another significance of the extensive deposits of fat is that these tissues being lighter than water, help to counteract the heaviness of the whale's body so that, with the assistance of the lungs, neutral buoyancy is achieved. The fat is accumulated between the muscle strands; in fact, in every available nook and cranny.

Food Storage

Some of this fat is drawn upon for food in time of need. Whenever a whale is existing on its fatty tissue,

acetone is one of the waste products which must be eliminated in the breath. This pungent material makes the breath strong and noticeable at these times.

Ordinarily, fatty tissues accumulate only when there is a surplus of food over the needs of the animal. You might suspect that whales would need to stockpile fat first, in order to remain warm and buoyant, and that growth would be curtailed and accomplished last. However, studies on the growth of whales show that the efficiency of food gathering is so high and food so plentiful that growth continues at a tremendous pace.

SEXUAL MATURITY AND REPRODUCTION

Whales mature sexually in approximately the eighth year. Toothed cetaceans, however, attain sexual maturity later than filter-feeding whales. A blue whale is sexually mature at 5 years, whereas porpoises require at least 7 years. Most filtering whales are sexually mature in 2 or 3 years. Whales, unlike most mammals, are not fully grown at sexual maturity but continue to grow for years. Female whales generally can be expected to produce a baby every other year, for the gestation period is approximately one year. Babies are nursed for 8 months. At birth the baby is completely formed and active, but lacking baleen must nurse. A blue whale baby at birth weighs approximately 8 tons, about 1/12th of the weight of the mother. The mother provides the baby with 50 gallons of milk a day. Since the nursing is done under water, and the baby must surface frequently to breathe, the act of nursing is very brief. Gray whale mothers nurse on their sides with one flipper extended into the air. To keep from being rolled as the baby places its muzzle into a mammary slit the mother may stabilize herself by placing her head on the flukes of another female who lies upside down with her flukes extended. This cooperative act is not often observed, however, and more commonly nursing occurs on slacktide at the edge of the channel where stabilization is possible. Muscles in the breasts of the mother force the milk into the baby's mouth in large amounts. The milk has the consistency of soft margarine and does not mix with the sea water which is ever present in the mouth. A muscular contraction in the tongue forces the milk into the throat for swallowing by confining it between the edges of the tongue and the roof of the mouth. The baby will double its length in 7 months, which averages to a daily weight gain of 220 pounds. During all this time the mother must fatten for the winter ahead and perhaps continue to grow herself.

LIFE SPAN

It is not known for certain how long a whale may live after completing its growth. At the present time, commercially important species seldom attain full physical maturity before being captured. Many whales which are captured are measured for scientific study. Whales apparently do not live to be very old. Fifty years appears to be the best current estimate of a life span.

At the present time very few gray whales have reached full physical maturity, and the death rate in the lagoons and along the migration path is confined mostly to babies and yearlings. In time, however, whalers permitting, more whales will reach physical maturity and die of natural causes.

WHALE INTELLIGENCE

Whales are apparently very intelligent animals. Whalers have remarked how difficult it is to approach whales which have previously escaped. Gray whales have been observed actually avoiding the coast after shore whaling had been carried out for a few seasons. The elaborate verbalizations of toothed whales have produced speculation among psychologists that they might have a language. Efforts to decipher this were not particularly fruitful. The employment of toothed whales to work for the Navy by having them retrieve, deliver or destruct objects is an extension of the food-bond technique of animal trainers. The animal can manage to display a long sequence of behaviorisms which appear nothing short of miraculous.

WHALE SENSES

Sight

Certainly the eyes are very important. It is not likely that the eye is very effective out of water even though whales do elevate the head out of the water for a look around. The behavior has been appropriately called "spyhopping" and it is manifested usually in the ice floes. Killer whales are believed to search the sea's surface and the edge of the icebergs for seals and birds. Visibility in ocean water varies markedly depending upon the amounts and kinds of suspended microscopic and macroscopic plants and animals, and debris. Visibility of more than a hundred feet is exceptional except far from land. The placement of the eyes on the sides of the head, well back from the tip of the jaws, prevent viewing directly ahead. The angle of viewing must be narrow judging from the fact that the whale rolls over on its side to look down or up. The characteristic swing of the head by yawing may connote forward inspection. Baby gray whales manifest much visual curiosity above the surface of the water. They constantly elevate their head out of the water by sliding up over the back of the mother, particularly when the mother is asleep and is approached by boat. The act of breaching which carries the whales' eyes 30 feet or more into the air is often done under conditions of limited visibility, especially in those locations where hearing is often blocked by extraneous noise or unfamiliar obstacles such as a jetty or sand bar.

Hearing

Whales appear to have very acute hearing. The report of a whaling gun will alarm whales which have previously tolerated a nearby whaling vessel. Fortunately for whales, water is a medium in which sound is transmitted for long distances. Whales not only have a keen sense of hearing, but also a sophisticated sound emitting system. It is this system of sonar that permits the gray whale to traverse the turbid waters of the lagoons without danger of stranding and to locate concentrations of food at a distance of a mile or two.

In recent times navies of several nations have been alarmed by unidentified underwater objects which cannot easily be distinguished from submarines. Some of these contacts are produced by whales. The counter measures not only cost the whale its life, but also causes the navies unnecessary expenditures of depth charges and time, and produce considerable tension and anxiety. There is a continual chatter among members of a porpoise school, or gam, as the whalers call them. The accumulated noise serves as a beacon to which straying members can home when they have gotten out of visual range. No one yet knows exactly how these animals can produce these sounds without being able to move air across the vocal chords. The toothed cetaceans which are gregarious are capable of a great variety of vocalizations.

Smell-Touch-Taste

The sense of smell is not important to whales, and the organ was abandoned when the nostrils were shifted to the back of the head and modified for diving. It is doubtful that the sense of taste plays much of a role for whales. They are not carrion feeders so the danger of ingesting poisonous byproducts of decay are slight. Sense of touch appears important to baby whales which keep in contact with their mothers bodies, and captive whales like to be caressed. Whalers on the other hand considered touch to be nonexistent since the harpooned whale did not react to the prick of the harpoon until it felt the pull of the restraining line. The one exception to their observations was the California gray whale which reacted instantly to the harpoon by rolling onto its side to strike its adversary.

They clearly recognize the environmental signposts which guide them to and from their various areas.

Oceanographers are not nearly as adept in recognizing these cues. Whales clearly recognize their own particular kind and they do not intermingle.

SOCIAL HABITS

Filtering whales, unlike the gregarious porpoises and dolphins, seldom school. Even when they appear to be abundant in a limited area they have congregated for feeding and not for social interaction. Toothed cetaceans, on the other hand, are generally sociable. The sperm whale travels in large groups of females dominated by a single bull whale. The other males have been driven away and the victorious male exercises control of the harem only as long as he wins these contests. Once the dominant male is defeated he becomes a solitary individual.

ENEMIES

Killer Whales

There have been isolated reports of killer whales attacking, and occasionally killing the gray whale. The gray whale is described as being very disturbed whenever a killer whale appears. On the coast of Siberia the gray whale will hide in very shallow water and if cornered is said to go into shock, floating at the surface, stomach up, while the killer whale bites at the tongue and flippers. Perhaps reports like this have been improperly interpreted. It is easy to understand how killer whales would congregate around the catch of the whaler. Recently studies on the loss of hooked tunas from the

The killer whale, is identified by its bold black and white markings and large dorsal fin. It is seen here in the spyhopping position, presumably having a look around. While not much is known about vision in larger whales, the small ones are known to have keen eyesight in and out of water. Killer whales grow to about 32 ft. and can weigh 10 tons.

long-line fishery of the Japanese, show that killer whales are adept at stealing fish along the setline. Additional studies on the natural history of the killer whale must be made before its relationship to other whales can be properly assessed.

Other Enemies

Other predators have left their marks on an occasional cetacean. For example, the Pacific lamprey at times attaches itself to a gray whale, to feed upon its blood, leaving a telltale scar. A bottlenose dolphin has been found freshly dead with a circular patch of its fluke removed, obviously by a large shark. Of course, man is a prime enemy of some cetaceans.

Parasites

If whales generally lead a charmed life with respect to predators, they still have their share of parasites, both external and internal. Their huge bodies are ideal platforms for the growth of barnacles which have specialized for this unusual habitat. Another very annoying skin parasite is the whale louse, which is a small flattish crustacean that clings by claws to the delicate skin. The digestive tract of the whale provides a wonderful habitat for round worms and tapeworms. Like their host, these parasites are the largest of their kind. Other organs such as the kidneys, liver and lungs may also be infested.

Ambergris

Sperm whales suffer from another affliction which is an obstruction of the intestine by a fatty concretion which forms from the bile. Ordinarily this is passed from the digestive tract when small, but if it is retained and continues to grow, an obstruction is possible. The material is grayish wax known as ambergris. It is used by the perfume industry to make permanent blends of various fragrances. Most of this material is obtained by whalers when they process the sperm whale. Only rarely does the material float ashore after the death of the unfortunate producer. Nowadays the value of ambergris is but moderate.

WHALE DEFORMITIES

Whales are found with healed broken bones which must have been incurred by fighting and other collisions. The skin of whales is mottled with scars which were produced by parasites and by fighting. Toothed whales are especially scarred from the raking by the teeth of an adversary during battles of dominance.

Now and then whales are born with birth defects—vestigial hind legs. Whales are sighted crippled with tail flukes partially or totally missing. Collisions with ships at night, which are not always fatal, are believed responsible. Injured skin of whales repairs itself with white scar tissue and the kinds of injuries can be read from pattern of scars. Barnacles, lice, lampreys, hagfish all leave a characteristic scar. The most celebrated abnormality was the albino sperm whale fictionized by Melville in *Moby Dick*. Whalers do find, now and then, albino whales.

THE STUDY OF WHALES

Whales have been extensively described both in popular and scientific writings. However, these accounts are by no means complete or necessarily correct. It will be many years before all the information can be obtained on these animals which range the wide oceans where man must study them under great disadvantage. Long term observations at sea are costly, and one has the problem of maintaining contact at night, during periods of fog, and during periods of windy weather when the whale's spout is easily missed. Until man has the underwater mobility and maneuverability of whales, he will have to be content with surmise and interpretations based on limited observations.

Much is known about the anatomy and fine structure of whales. One can certainly admire the work of the early anatomists who persevered in dissecting the partially decomposed carcasses of stranded specimens. What a contrast to the opportunity afforded now to the anatomist who need merely be present on a whaling ship to receive any part which he wishes to examine. It takes the whaling ship 4 to 6 hours to butcher a whale completely.

Naturally, the whales which are currently the object of research are those which are commercially important and available. The dynamics of whale populations is the most pressing problem. The California gray whale which would be convenient for study is no longer taken commercially. Permission would have to be obtained from the International Whaling Commission to secure even a single specimen, and a scientist could not easily obtain a specimen without the assistance of whalers. Fortunately, we know a great deal about the species as a result of an extensive monograph prepared nearly 100 years ago by Captain C. M. Scammon, who was among the first to whale for this animal commercially. Professor Edward D. Cope described the species, giving it the name *Rhachianectes glauca,* after he examined a skeleton which had been shipped to him at the Academy of Natural Sciences of Philadelphia.

Roy Chapman Andrews of the American Museum of Natural History prepared the first detailed description of a specimen which he found at a Korean whaling station in the winter of 1911-12. At the time of his report the species had not been seen for many years and had been believed extinct. More recently Russian scientists published considerable material which they had obtained from Russian whalers who had continued to harvest this species during the thirties of this century. They studied the food of this whale in detail, and clearly showed that the herd that summered in the Sea of Okhotsk and wintered off Korea (and still does so in limited numbers) did not intermingle with the Bering Sea herd which wintered in the lagoons of Baja California. Since 1937 the species has enjoyed protection from whaling on an international basis. Beginning in 1947 whaling scientists of the Canadian and American fishery agencies have published data principally on the recovery of the California herd, and to a degree have filled in some of the gaps in its life history. Recent studies of Rice and Wolman demonstrate that the California gray whale is

"It should be kept in mind that this whale is regarded as the most primitive
of the living baleen-bearing whales, and it seems to represent the stage
in the evolutionary sequence from which the two main groups diverged."

quite similar in many of its biological details to those which appear in the commercially important species.

In American waters whales are protected by the Marine Mammal Act, as specified within the 12 mile limit. A permit to collect specimens for marine parks or research is required and whales cannot be harassed by whale watchers.

ALIFORNIA GRAY WHALE

Evolutionary Areas

It should be kept in mind that this whale is regarded as the most primitive of the living baleen-bearing whales, and it seems to represent the stage in the evolutionary sequence from which the two main groups diverged. The California gray whale is the sole survivor of a family of whales which in past eons was represented by many species. It has a smallish head with a limited filtering mechanism. Its dependence on foods that are found only near shore is considered further evidence that it is primitive. Likewise its need for harbors to calve suggests that it has not lost its dependence on the nearshore habitat, even though it could safely cross the wide Pacific. The extremely restricted and separated

distribution pattern of the whale is typical of an old, primitive species which persists either in its preferred ancestral home, or which occupies less desirable habitats into which it was forced by the more successful species. It would appear logical to assume that the coastal habitat is the choicest in the ocean, and the gray whale by means of its diversified feeding continues to dominate even though this is a habitat of limited extent and contiguous to man. It may very well be that the conquest of the main bodies of the oceans by whales was an evolutionary event that required more specialized feeding mechanisms in order to survive in less productive habitats. In 1937 gray whale remains were found in the Netherlands, and it is possible that it was exterminated in European waters by prehistoric whaling in postglacial time.

Geographic Distribution

It is evident that the gray whale is now confined to the Pacific sector, reaching its northern limits in the ice floes of the Arctic Ocean and it is assumed that there are two residual populations. One population, by far the larger, summers and feeds largely in Bering Sea, though some are now being found to occur in summer in cold coastal waters south even as far as northern California. This group breeds in late winter and spring very largely in Scammons Lagoon (Laguna Ojo de Liebre complex) and  other lagoons farther south in central Baja California, Mexico, and thence southward through the Bahia

Some typical migration activities of the California gray whale are seen here. In the background the sequence of events in surfacing, blowing and diving is seen. Observers of the gray have noted a relationship between the length of a dive and the number of blows. A single blow indicates a one minute dive, two blows, two minutes, etc.

Mating activity is seen in the foreground. Precopulatory behavior is often lengthy, requiring sufficient contact by the males to arouse the females.

In the initial aspects of mating (left), a female is flanked by two coaxing males which have crowded in alongside. She has already made her prenuptial roll, breaching the surface and turning over on her back into a receptive position. One of the males (right) successfully mounts the female while the other trails along with the copulating pair. The mating position shown here is typical.

Magdalena complex north of Cabo San Lucas. A few move far up the Gulf of California and rather small groups breed along the east side of the Gulf. A few young are born off southern California.

The second population, generally thought to be quite independent, summers in Okhotsk Sea west of Kamchatka and the Kurile chain of islands. This is the group that supported Korean whaling in the western part of the sea of Japan during the early decades of this century, and Japanese scientists believe that gray whales formerly moved down the east side of Japan and wintered in the Inland Sea. For some time in more recent years, it was commonly assumed that the Asiatic herd had become extinct, but Russian marine mammalogists, including some working in Vladivostok, have now found that a few members of the Asiatic herd still survive.

Since the 1850's there have been three brief periods of whaling for the gray whale in the eastern north Pacific, the last in the 1939's, each separated by about 20 years. Each succeeding period of whaling has been shorter, suggesting that 20 years might not be a long enough period for recovery. At present, commercial operations on the gray whale are prohibited by international agreement and it seems certain that any proposal for resumption of the commercial kill would meet with intense and widespread opposition.

Shore Habits

Generally speaking, shallow water seems to be dangerous for the larger whales, other than the gray and right whales. Other species do actually strand, but perhaps only under abnormal conditions. Gray whales manage to swim in very shallow water. They have been seen rolling in the surf in water barely deep enough to float them. In the lagoons they negotiate the seemingly treacherous turbid channels, notwithstanding the strength of the tidal currents.

At the present time it is difficult to understand why the lagoons are used by the gray whale for calving. It presumably is an ancestral behavior trait that has been inherited. The quiet waters facilitate birth and nursing during the time the baby is gaining strength for the long migration. The term "quiet," however, is misleading as usually a tidal current of 2 to 3 knots keeps the visibility less than 5 feet. The interplay of tidal current and wind

produce a surface chop which seems to make breathing difficult for the infant whale. To compound the difficulties the uppermost reaches of the tidal channels carry water which has twice the salinity of ocean water. Whales must be able to excrete the extra burden of salt. One theory supposes that the additional buoyancy makes it easier for the baby whale to stay at the surface until it gains enough fat to float. However, the adults must adjust this unneeded ballast by exhaling sizable volumes of air to dive against the current.

The lagoons are supposed to provide an ideal place for the birth and growth of the baby. If so, the lagoons must be a mixed blessing because the water is so turbid as to afford less than 10 feet of visibility and usually the water is flowing in or out in response to the tidal effect at velocities of 1 to 3 knots. Depth fluctuates from six to eight feet to create potential danger of stranding, particularly to babies and juveniles.

The whales generally congregate in the innermost regions when the tides are at flood and maximum. Conversely the whales vacate these areas before the tide ebbs. The movement of whales within the lagoon does not always coincide with a favorable current. It may proceed against the current obliquely, much as a sailboat tacks. If a whale tends to stay in a particular area it will move into the lee of a sandbar, tidal islet, or the convergence of two tidal channels.

As the tide begins to pass over the whale at the end of the slack-water period they orient directly into the current and hold position by diving to the bottom, then rolling over onto their side to leave the fluke half out of the water and vertical. As the front of the tidal current advances as a tidal bore, it puts into counter motion each and every whale it passes.

From time to time whales surface upside down with the tail flukes against the bottom. The tidal current levers the whale's head into a vertical position, reminiscent of a navigational spar. Whalers designated this posture as "spy-out." To regain the horizontal position the tail is released and whale's head settles into water and the whale rolls over, surfaces and takes a breath.

One may wonder whether the lagoons, which are limited in number and in extent, may control the size of the population. Lagoons are subject to change in size and depth through geologic processes and they may be

With its tail flukes braced against the lagoon floor, this gray whale has taken the spar position against the tidal surge. With this maneuver the whale avoids having to continuously swim against the tidal current while in shallow water. The coarse spotted appearance of the whale is produced by numerous barnacles adhered to its skin. In addition, the whale's skin provides a home for sharp-clawed crustaceans known as whale lice.

created or destroyed. One may also wonder whether the whales would continue to use them if they were also much used by man. Scammon's Lagoon is flanked by evaporation ponds to make salt which is transferred by barge to Cedros Island for loading on ships. In spite of barge shipments night and day, whales continue to use the lagoon. The vastness and beauty of the surrounding desert dunes and the winter occupancy by the whale have prompted the Mexican government to proclaim Scammon's Lagoon (Laguna Ojo de Liebre) a National Park.

Scientific Description

The California gray whale was believed initially to be a Pacific species. On that assumption, Cope (1869) prepared a description and gave it a scientific name unaware that the paleontologist Lilljeborg had described a collection of fossil bones of the same type of whale from the Atlantic. It was not until 1937 that Van Deinse and Junge discovered that this collection was none other than the California gray whale. Since Lilljeborg's description precedes Cope's, the name presently in use is *Eschrichtius robustus*, the name given by Lilljeborg.

Reaction to Whaling

The California gray whale is known by other common names, such as "koku kujira" of the Japanese, which means "devil fish." This indicates the cleverness of the gray whale and the dangers associated with hunting it. Whalers universally considered this species the most difficult to whale and the only one which might charge the boat. Gray whales certainly seemed to learn quickly the dangers to them from whaling. Captain Scammon considered this species the most interesting, giving it top billing in his book on the Mammals of the Pacific Coast. He reports that it was standard practice in the lagoons to kill the baby in order to lure the mother into harpoon range. In these encounters, the whalers showed great courage standing the charge of the angry mother as they took a chance of losing their boats and their lives. The females of other whale species have a strong maternal instinct, but none of them seems to be so consistently willing to fight for its young as the gray whale.

We still do not know much about the behavior of the gray whale or the other filtering whales. At present, the people who are best informed on this subject are the whalers. They can ill afford to waste valuable time trailing whales which are too wary to be approached. In general, feeding whales are easiest to approach, being intent on feeding and completely oblivious to the approach of a whaling vessel. Feeding whales, although oblivious to the approach of the whaler, do not surface with any degree of regularity and the point of emergence cannot be predicted so it was necessary to frighten the whale with a loud noise to put it into flight. The whale is then pursued until tiring when it travels without diving deeply. Then its course can be predicted and the whaling vessel can hasten to bring itself within harpoon range. This procedure was called galling a whale. Ordinarily, once harpooned, a whale attempts to escape its tormentors rather than turn and demolish the boat, which of course, would have put an early end to whaling. In the instances of a whale ramming a boat, it is usually an accident, occurring during the death flurry. However, there are exceptions, and of course these make whaling hazardous.

Sleeping Whales

One question about whale behavior that remains somewhat unanswered is—how much rest do whales require? There have been indications that the California gray whale in the lagoons of Baja California may frequently rest. They can be observed apparently sleeping for periods up to one hour. Only a small sliver of the mid-back region breaks the surface, and the head and the tail hang down. Every five minutes the head is elevated slightly to clear the blowhole for breathing. The drooping tail prevents the whale from drifting into too shallow water on a flooding tide. There is no vapor in the breath at this time so that it is difficult to find the whale unless one is close.

A mother asleep may have a seemingly fretful baby that circles her, often running up onto her flank to expose its head. As soon as one approaches the pair the baby

becomes agitated and strikes the head of the mother to awaken her. To get underway the female slips backward to tilt the head clear of the water for a look and then quickly

exits. Sleeping follows several hours of what the author interprets as feeding. Cinematic record of a whale seemingly falling asleep has been made.

Migrating whales have been followed for 12 hours of the 13 hours of daylight without a nap. What happens after dark is a matter of real importance to the scientists responsible for the census of the gray whale. Presently the count is multiplied by two to account for those which are believed to pass by at night. Navy scientists working contiguous with the census station note that the gray whales are nearly as noisy at night as by day. Furthermore they theorize that these low frequency sounds are directive and permit migration at night. In support of this opinion are observations made from ships anchored in the path of the migration, that whales can be heard blowing as they pass. On the other hand the author using the most sophisticated infrared scanners operating from an aircraft flying repeatedly over the same area rarely noted signs of swimming.

Dr. Carl L. Hubbs observed gray whales migrating southward off Pt. Loma on a phenomenally quiet sea, under full, bright moonlight, in the very same pattern followed during the day. A Navy research submarine has also secured evidence by sonar of whales passing La Jolla in quite regular fashion from before to shortly after sundown. Thereafter, until nearly midnight sonar failed to give evidence of the continuing migration. Until low frequency sound emanations are unequivocally established as navigational it is best to consider the matter open for further study.

Migration Groupings

The California gray whale is not believed to be particularly gregarious. The groupings observed at the lagoons are thought to be due to the limited areas that are available for mating and calving. There is some indication that they form groups during their migrations. Russian observers say that early in autumn groups gather and start out on the migration. The Japanese have noted groups of moderate size remaining together during the crossing of Bering Sea. As yet no one has attempted to trail a group of grays along the entire migration route. Not only would this establish the route, but also add to our knowledge about their behavior en route.

At San Diego three categories of migrants have been observed on the southward migration. During the early and middle periods of the migration, many solitary whales are seen. These are believed to be pregnant

In apparent serenity this California gray moves silently past blades of giant kelp in its underwater world. Its annual migrations to the lagoons of Baja California bring it close to the shoreline in many places. This makes whale-watching a favorite activity among local residents and visitors alike.

31

Having blundered
into an offshore kelp bed,
this gray breaches the surface in a tangle of giant

kelp. This kind of prob-
lem is usually avoided,
but grays have been seen
spyhopping through the
massive kelp beds as they
seek clear water. It is generally the young, inex-
perienced traveler that
runs into obstacles in its
first migration.

females. They travel at about 4 knots and surface frequently, about every 3 minutes. The migrating groups of three to five are made up of one or more nonpregnant females accompanied by one or more males. These are often courting. At any rate, the migration is less hurried, and the individuals spend much time on the surface, blowing and milling about. Such groups are seen principally during the middle part of the migration and they are easiest to sight. They afford the spectators at Cabrillo National Monument quite a show. Not infrequently, these groups put on a display for an hour or two.

Toward the end of a season one sees migrants that are smaller and closer to shore just outside the kelp beds. These are believed to be last year's young, making the trip alone for the first time. They not only swim more slowly, but they also seem to wander into the kelp and into every irregularity of the coast. Those which enter the kelp may raise the head vertically out of the water in an action called spyhopping. They are obviously trying to find a passage through the kelp. The fact that the gray whale does not spyhop regularly on its migration along the shore must mean that its orientation is based either on the sound of the surf or the depth of the water. Spyhopping is apparently employed by the whales in the lagoons, and it has been observed frequently for the other species in the ice floes of the polar seas.

Mating

It is difficult to observe all the details of courtship. The courting whales roll over in the water extending the flippers alternately like spars. Mating generally takes place near the lagoons and also in the lower ends of the lagoons.

Recent studies of Rice and Wolman covered the dissection of 316 gray whales collected off San Francisco. To account for two sizes of embryos they postulated that the females first ovulate in November so that most matings occur to the north but that if the female is not mated, or if the mating is infertile, she will ovulate a second time in 40 days. Matings that are observed farther south in January probably are of this category. Gestation period is calculated to be 13 months, so births occur mainly in January when the expectant female has reached the lagoon, but may continue well into February.

Observations conducted from ship and from helicopter by the author indicate the usual sequence of events during matings. Because the whales sink out of sight now and then, the below-water events described are believed to be a continuation of those in progress at the surface.

At the beginning of courtship the female swims evasively with one to seven males in pursuit. Gradually the males drop out, until normally two remain. By now the female has slowed and the males crowd her flanks. The female surfaces upside down spiralling. The males swim up onto the body of the female, grazing her genital area. Next, the female stops swimming and may be rolled over by the attempt of the males to mount. The males flank the female on either side clasping her body with their flippers to stop the rolling. The tail area of the female is forced down by the weight of the males. This causes her to pivot her head up out of the water and then to sink tail first. The heads of the males also break water whenever they slide up onto her body. Considering the size of the whales, the gentleness of contact is amazing. Except for rolling, the movements are reminiscent of a slow motion film. The males may follow the female as she dives vertically downward, exposing their tails which wave to and fro. When the female is thoroughly aroused she lies at the surface upside down with her flippers extended. The males swim upside down along side with their intromittent organs exposed. The organ is curved and sufficiently long to reach across the not inconsiderable girth of the female to touch her midsection. The two males will adjust their position to contact the female's genital opening. There is also some positioning of the genital organ by extension and rotation. As soon as the genital organs are in contact the pair roll toward each other to complete the coupling. The separation of the pair does not necessarily connote the end of courtship, as the threesome will stay together throughout at least that day. It is remarkable that a pair of males can function without belligerence, content to leave to chance their ultimate participation, although a single male can effect a mating taking a longer time. Often a third or fourth, usually smaller male, may be noted just outside the mating area (curiosity or the first manifestations of sex?).

''Whales may breach more than once, and in fact, one was observed
to jump repeatedly, as many as 25 times within an hour's
passing of the Point Loma area.''

Breaching

Occasionally the gray whale bursts out of the water at about a 45 degree angle, usually to turn over, falling back with a tremendous splash. This is called breaching, and its significance is not known. It is frequently displayed by solitary migrants. Whales may breach more than once, and in fact, one was observed to jump repeatedly, as many as 25 times within an hour's passing of the Point Loma area. Here one or two migrants are apt to breach each week. Unfortunately, the act takes place so quickly that often the final splash is all that is seen or only a quick glimpse of the whale's massive body. However, this sight repays many hours of patient watching. Should water be noted streaming from the mouth the author concludes that the breaching was made through a school of fish, and that the drainage of the water is preparatory to swallowing.

In the lagoons whales breach at the entrance more than within the lagoon. The water there is extremely turbid and saturated with noise from the breakers that flank the entrance. About double the normal frequency of breaching has been noted when sailing counter to the migrating whales. The passage of low flying aircraft appears to put the animals into breaching one time per whale, as the plane passes over the lagoon. One can cause whales to breach around a jetty or breakwater, providing one herds the whale to stay inside of it. Suddenly encountering acoustically an unfamiliar obstacle appears to generate a breach. I postulate that breaching in these instances is due to the failure of the acoustic ranging, and that the breach is a means of ascertaining what lies ahead. An unexpected breach has been filmed which appeared to be a response to a mother and calf passing in front of the breacher. Lastly, whales may breach to dislodge vexatious lice, and gulls will follow a whale that is so involved, to feed on the lice.

''The ideal approach to a whale is from behind
with the vessel running only slightly faster than the whale,
so that the approach is gradual.''

**HALE**

WATCHING FROM SHIPS OR BOATS

Sportfishing vessels feature whale watching trips
of two to three hours duration to bring the whale
watcher within a few hundred feet of the migrant whale.
Numerous whale watchers who own their own boats also
find trailing whales exciting.

Anyone contemplating taking up this sport or wishing
to improve skill in the approach should remember that
there is associated with the boat's passage through the
water a broad spectrum of sound made by the friction of
boat's hull plus noises transmitted into the water through
the hull, footsteps, dropped articles, and the engines and
propeller sounds. When the propeller turns rapidly

''white noise'' is made by the release of air from water in
contact with propeller. The noise envelope radiates out
from the ship and, if it is excessive, the whale will
attempt to keep clear, either by speeding up or turning.

Once this happens, it is better to search for a new
group, hopefully far enough removed from other vessels
to involve solo contact. The ideal approach to a whale is
from behind with the vessel running only slightly faster
than the whale, so that the approach is gradual. When the
approach is properly made, the whale or whales may
slow down and surface abeam for a look at the boat.

In contemplating whale watching with one's own boat
or with friends, there are a number of considerations. It
is essential to always approach whales from astern. It is
undesirable to tag along a boat already following a
whale. Commonly whales nearest to port are being
followed by an excursion vessel. The collective noise
generated by a small armada of well-meaning whale
watchers prevents the whales from hearing each other

This scenario depicts several aspects of the gray whale's behavior. The scene is one of the shallow lagoons in the Gulf of California. At the left, a gray is making a complete breach, its heavy body driven upward by powerful fluke movements. Gray's may breach during feeding, if acoustical ranging fails, while dislodging ecto-parasites, and when disturbed. At the left foreground, a mother swims along with her calf partially supported on her flipper. In this position, the calf's forward movement may be assisted by the slipstream produced by the mother. At center foreground, a gray plows through the muddy bottom as it sucks crustaceans into its mouth. Following this it will eject water and debris through its baleen plates, trapping the food within. Bottom feeding in this manner is common among grays.

At the right foreground a gray maintains the spar position, its flukes resting on the lagoon floor and its back to the current. To the center background, in deeper water, another gray is seen spyhopping. With its head above the surface, it scans its surroundings. While the shallow lagoons are a place of constant jeopardy for the big mammals, they return to these waters with dependable regularity. Here the calves are born and reared in preparation for their long northern migration to the summer feeding grounds.

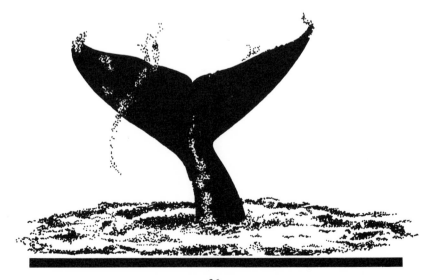

and they will attempt to evade the boats. Once this happens inexperienced boat operators will speed to the surfacing site only to frighten the whales, which are prevented from inhaling an adequate number of breaths. That whale will never allow another close, intimate look.

The Marine Act enacted by Congress specifically protects marine mammals from harassment and makes it a misdemeanor to harass or otherwise disturb whales in our coastal waters. Knowing this, a boat operator should proceed either northward or southward sufficiently far to find another, not yet closely followed, group.

The majority of owners of pleasure craft operate their vessels during daylight. There is some danger of colliding with a whale when traveling close to shore at night.

Watching From Land

The selection of the place from which to watch whales is based on two requirements: that the whales are passing close enough to be easily sighted and that the viewer is sufficiently elevated to be able to look down and over the sea surface. The headland coast provides promontories terminating in seacliffs from which a near aerial view can be had.

Recommended Areas for Observing Migrating Gray Whales
CANADA:
Queen Charlotte Islands (west coast)
Vancouver Island (west coast): Provincial State Park at Long Beach. A few nonmigrating whales are present here the year around.

UNITED STATES:
Washington:
Cape Flattery to Cape Alava Olympic National Park, La Push, Queets (whales tarry at mouths of all rivers emptying into the sea).
Oregon:
Columbia River, as well as all other river mouths.
Seal Rocks
California:
Northern California river mouths
Point Reyes National Sea Shore
Fort Ross State Historic Monument
Point Lobos State Reserve
Monterey/Carmel Area
San Simeon coast along State Highway 1
Morro Bay
Montana de Oro State Park
La Jolla
Cabrillo National Monument, San Diego

BAJA CALIFORNIA:
Coronado Islands
Punta Banda (Ensenada)
San Martin Island
Santo Tomas Point
Scammon's Lagoon
Magdalena Bay
Cabo San Lucas

Note: Wherever mountains meet the sea the coastal cliffs are ideal for whale watching. Unfortunately, such areas are not usually traversed by good roads. Where deep water comes close to land, whales, particularly young ones, follow the submarine canyons, often practically to the beach. The California State Parks provide an interpretive program at those sites where whales can be sighted. Los Angeles County maintains a museum at Portuguese Bend. Whale-watching excursion boats operate from San Diego, Dana Point, Newport Beach, Long Beach, and Ventura.

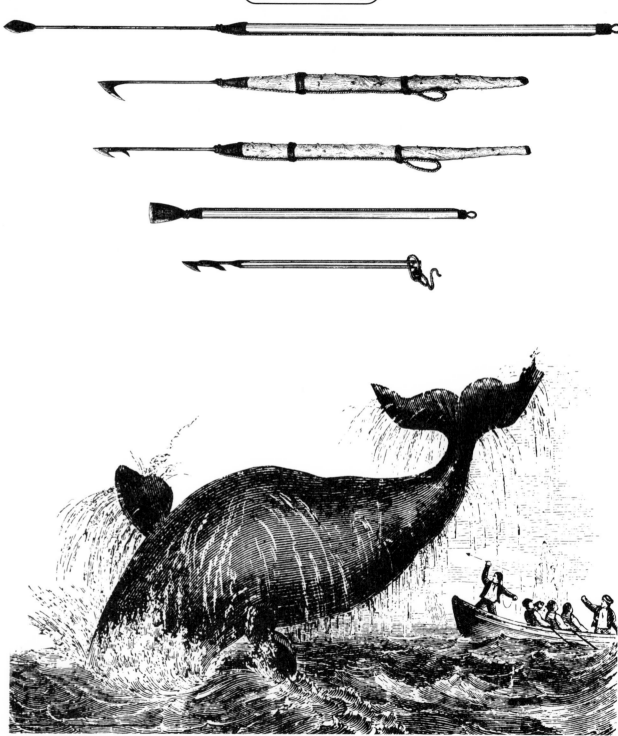

WHALING

The role that whaling has played in man's conquest of the oceans has never been given full credit by historians (although, for the gray whale, this question has been treated in depth by David A. Henderson). Initially man was content to fish along the shore and then he gradually pushed out on the waters in sight of land. Here he learned to be a skilled fisherman, and he began to hunt the coastal whales. Man gradually developed the boats, gear, seamanship, and gained the courage to venture farther and farther from land. Even as late as the 15th century sailors were extremely superstitious and believed in sea monsters. There was, of course, a certain basis for these imaginings. Periodically, a large whale would strand or float ashore and it is easy to understand how these tremendous and misshapen remains could have kindled the imagination. Whaling was an extremely hazardous profession calling for the utmost in nautical skill. Throughout the development of the maritime resources of some European states whaling was one of their most profitable businesses. Even though much shipbuilding was initiated by man's speculative desire to find new lands and to conduct trade an equal amount was provided for whaling vessels. From the Middle Ages to nearly the end of the 19th century oil from whales illuminated many homes and streets. Whale meat was an important source of protein for peoples who had not yet developed extensive animal husbandry.

For over five centuries whales have been under attack by professional hunters, and long before that by aboriginal peoples of many lands. The reason whales have withstood this hunting pressure better than land animals is that their ocean habitat has been little utilized by man for aquaculture. In the days of sailing ships and hand harpooning the whale was a formidable prey, far more so than in the present day of motorization and automation. The tremendous area of their habitat made it difficult and time consuming for man to find them, and his ignorance of their migration routes and the oceanographic features that cause whales to disperse and congregate gave the whales some protection. Technological advances, powerful harpoon guns and totally mechanized factory ships in the whaling industry have swung the advantage to man, and whales are now in a state of near extinction as is the whaling industry itself.

Whalers as Explorers

History tends to stress the great explorers who discovered new worlds and the larger islands of the Pacific. However, ships cannot with full safety ply the seven seas until every island and shoal has been found and charted, and ships cannot safely venture near any shore until the adjoining waters have been systematically charted. The principal discoverers of these danger spots have been the whalers who patiently combed so much of the oceans in their search for whales. Every island has on it the calling cards of whalers who put ashore for water, food, fuel, or just to stretch their legs and to satisfy their curiosity. This isn't to say that they had the time to make hydrographic surveys, but at least their log books defined the areas where surveys would eventually have to be made. Whalers lived adventure, and danger was their common lot. It is not surprising that much of this adventure would find its way into the hearts of men through yarns and tales such as Moby Dick.

Early Whaling

Whaling was practiced prehistorically. The coastal Eskimos of the arctic Americas and of Greenland and Spitzbergen hunted whales. Whales were approached in skin-covered boats and even from the edge of ice floes. These peoples are differentiated ethnically on the basis of the variations in their whaling techniques, in their whaling gear and in their religious preparations for whaling. It took great courage to whale such frigid waters where an overturning meant death. It is not surprising that these peoples looked to supernatural deities who required a very complex ritual to insure a safe and successful hunt.

The principal method of hunting involved coming up alongside the whale so that the man in the bow, the whaling captain, could spear the chest. If he were lucky enough to drive the shaft between the ribs, the lung could be pierced and the whale would be mortally wounded. Each time the whale surfaced the boat would attempt

"Aleutian islanders prepared a poisonous coating
for the harpoon tip which was sufficiently toxic to kill the whale."

another approach and lancing. The stone tip of the lance was detachable, and when freed, led to an inverted sealskin float by a long line of twisted sinews. These floats marked the location of the whale during submergence. Eventually the whale, weakened by loss of blood and by fright, would die and then came the chore of hand pulling the whale ashore for feasting and reprovisioning the village's storehouses. The captain of the boat and his crew were considered the most skilled and important of the hunters. Whaling was an ancestral skill that was passed from generation to generation with great care. The villages could ill afford to lose their best men, or equipment which was difficult to make.

There are interesting variations to this method. Aleutian islanders prepared a poisonous coating for the harpoon tip which was sufficiently toxic to kill the whale. This was prepared from the deadly aconite by a secret process, depending upon the concentration of the alkaloid poison from the root. Eskimos from Greenland and Spitzbergen dried another secret coating on the harpoon tip which consisted of a bacterium which produced a fatal blood poisoning in the whale. In either method the whalers waited for the bloated carcass to surface and then they hauled it ashore for eating. Apparently the spoiled meat had no ill effects on these peoples, but of course, much of their food was spoiled during the summertime.

Much of the religion of these primitive peoples centered around the need of giving the whaler and his crewmen the necessary courage and confidence to perform this job. Religious ceremonies were held weeks before, and again after, every hunt. Some of the deities were whales, and whales also figure predominantly in many of their folk tales.

The European and American whalers came in direct contact with the Eskimos competing not only for whales,

but also for seals, walrus, and fur-bearing animals. Today, Eskimos use harpoon guns and sturdy wooden whale boats. However, the entire village still turns out to drag a whale ashore. Each village kills only what it requires for food and oil through the long arctic winter. They hunt the arctic bowhead whale, although the smaller white whale (beluga) is also hunted. The bowhead has never recovered from commercial whaling, even though it has been protected for years by the International Whaling Commission. The regulations, however, do not apply to the aborigines but their needs should not have prevented the whales from becoming plentiful again.

The Indians who occupy the coastal waters of South Alaska and British Columbia are excellent salmon fishermen, but do not whale even though they possess magnificent boats suitable for this. However, at the entrance to Puget Sound and south along the Olympic Peninsula lived Indians who hunted whales as recently as 50 years ago. They whaled in much the same way as did the early Eskimos, with detachable stonetipped lances and seal-skin floats. It is believed that the whale they hunted was the California gray. Boats were hewn from the massive trunks of cedars. From the bark and wiry branches, a tough flexible line was woven, strong enough to withstand the terrific pull of the whale. These Indians repeatedly lanced the whale until its death. The generation of Indians who know this skill is gone, and the present generation only remembers vaguely the tales of their parents and grandparents. The Washington State Historical Museum in Seattle has managed to interview the old-timers and collect their gear which is now on display there.

The Kamchadal and Chukchi eskimos whose villages looked out on the summer grounds of the gray whale were not inclined to whale. They did, however, feed on any that happened to wash ashore.

In this early engraving a stalwart soul is about to harpoon a narwhal. The flimsy kayak offered little protection against the thrashing flukes. Once the harpoon was driven home, both line and cask followed.

The cask acted as a marker buoy, permitting the harpoon wielder to withdraw and follow at a safe distance until the whale succumbed.

Historic Whaling

Commercial whaling began in Spain during the Middle Ages. At that time the black right whale was plentiful along the coast of the Basque province of Spain and it provided an ideal quarry because it could be sighted from lookout towers along the coast and it was not difficult to approach. Equally important, these whales floated at death so they could be pulled ashore. They were prized for their oil and meat, and for the baleen that was sold throughout Europe. The Biscayan whalers gradually reduced the local population of whales and began to range farther in their search. They came at last upon the haunts of another right whale which frequented the ice-filled seas of the North Atlantic. Since there was not a satisfactory method to preserve the meat it was thrown away.

There is an extensive and fascinating history of this early whaling but only the briefest outline can be mentioned here. Throughout the story there is a constant search for new whaling grounds to sustain operations and to meet the increased demand for whaling products. As the industry expanded it was forced to capture less desirable species because the other species could not hold up against the onslaught.

Other nations took up whaling and soon the English and Dutch had large fleets of ships manned by Basque whalers. These ships were based in Greenland and Spitzbergen. The irregular coastlines of these windswept lands provided many harbors in which shore whaling stations could be situated. The camps were well constructed, and daily during the arctic summer the ships put out for whales in waters which were rough, cluttered with icebergs and shrouded in fog. Naturally, under such difficult conditions, there was great loss of ships and men. The companies were not friendly with one another and periodically raided the shore camps of each other, stealing and burning supplies and buildings. Under normal circumstances such activities would have been

Whalebone provided a lucrative bonus to the early whaling companies. In this photo from the Pacific Whaling Co. of San Francisco, whalebone is seen drying in stacks near the wharf. The steam whaler, Orca is tied up at the right. Baleen plates were manufactured into corset stays, buggy whips, umbrella ribs and skirt hoops. At one time, whalebone brought $7.00 a pound. Eventually, spring steel was to replace whalebone in many of its uses.

provocative of war. However, since communications were poor and the countries concerned were preoccupied with colonizing America the situation took care of itself, for in time the whales diminished and the whaling companies failed.

Soon after this the colonists in America wrote to relatives in Europe about the richness of the country, not the least of its resources being the whales which spouted just off shore along the entire Eastern seaboard. Whaling companies were formed and these were concentrated along the New England coast. After the separation of the colonies from England, whaling developed locally with the ships which had been engaged in commerce between the colonies and the mother country. It did not take long to exhaust the populations of whales, so the whalers began to range afar.

This led to the discovery of the haunts of the sperm whale in the open oceans of the tropics and subtropics. Yankee ingenuity developed a new kind of whaling in which the whales were brought alongside the base ship for processing. It took a great deal of skill to strip the blanket of fat from a whale which was three-fourths submerged and pitching and rolling on the restless surface. The blubber, once removed, was hauled aboard and cooked in kettles to free the oil which was then placed in barrels and stowed below. This form of whaling was called pelagic whaling. It was not uncommon for ships to be away from home port for a year or two before the casks were full. This whaling was dominated by the Americans, and it contributed much to the prosperity of New England, providing much of the capital which later financed its manufacturing developments. This was the golden era of whaling so superbly described by Herman Melville in *Moby Dick*. Here is a real yarn about whaling written by a whaler who later became a superb author.

The discovery of petroleum in Pennsylvania brought to the fore new illuminating fuels, kerosene and natural gas which were much cheaper than whale oil, so the whaling industry declined rapidly. This happened at the same time steam ships were replacing sailing ships, so it is not surprising that the beautiful sailing vessels which had been the mainstay of whaling were brought home to every little coastal village in New England to rot away, sad memorials to better days.

Modern Whaling

By the 20th century whaling was again possible because of new markets for whaling products. Chemistry has succeeded in finding new uses for whale oil. Fat derivatives such as soaps, margarines and a few other products owe their abundance and low cost to the whaling industry. Packing house technology has been applied to the butchering of whales so that the entire animal has many uses. Tasty meats are finding their way into the diets of many countries and the tougher, less tasty parts are ground and used to feed cats and dogs. Farms that raise mink and other mammals for the fur trade are heavy buyers of this source of meat to feed their animals. The remaining parts, blood, bones, and meat scraps, are dried and ground into nutritious meals which are used by the poultry and livestock industries as supplementary feeds. Currently each whale produces over $9,000 worth of products.

The heart of the processing operation is the pelagic factory ship which is nearly as large as an aircraft carrier. They are supplied by huge tankers which carry off the oil and by refrigerated ships which return the meat to port. In the 20th century the United States has not seriously participated in whaling and has not a single fleet in competition with the other countries, which now have billion dollar investments in ships and gear. For 70 years, the leader in the whaling industry was Norway. The industry is very competitive, however, and the major whaling countries are now the Soviet Union and Japan. Nearly all other countries that once whaled have ceased.

The Norwegian leadership was due principally to Svend Foyn, who invented the harpoon with an explosive head. The harpoon was fired by a deck-mounted cannon and it had sufficient range and accuracy to permit killing those whales which heretofore were too fast and wary to be hand-lanced. The harpoon head had a time delay bomb which insured that the explosion occurred deep in the vitals, and that the whale was made fast to a manila line so that it would not be lost. The cannon is mounted in the bow of a small fast ship known as a killer boat. These little ships operate for 1 or 2 days away from the factory ship in search of whales. The gunner who is responsible for firing the cannon is the most important member of the crew and on his

Shore stations like this one at Moss Landing, California were constructed to handle offshore whaling. The chunks of blubber seen here were processed for their oil which was then sold for lighting fuel. An average bowhead yielded 100 barrels (31.5 gal. each) while the gray yielded 25. Whale oil was an important fuel until replaced by petroleum in the early 1900's.

experience and skill depend the entire operation. If he misses or fails to kill the whale, it will alarm the other whales and a day or two of searching may have been in vain.

The whaling season is extremely short and as soon as the yearly quota has been reached all countries must stop. Naturally every whaling country has tried to get as many whales of the total as possible. Once a whale is killed it is hauled alongside and the body cavity is inflated with compressed air to make the whale buoyant. It should be remembered that the whales which are now being processed are the ''wrong'' not the right whales and they would otherwise sink. The whale is then flagged, lighted, and a radio transmitter secured to it, and it is cast adrift while the killer boat continues to search for more victims. At the end of the hunting period the killer boat retraces its route, picking up the whales it has killed. These are secured to the sides of the ship and brought back to the factory ship for processing.

Naturally, the technological improvements that made whaling profitable would have been meaningless without the discovery of new whaling grounds. About 1900 the seas around the Antarctic continent were found to be teeming with whales. These were principally four species—the humpback, the finback, the blue, and the minke. The blue whale is distinguished by the fact that it is the largest mammal on earth, reaching sometimes 100 feet in length and weighing over 100 tons. It has been the species long preferred by whalers but it is not as plentiful as its close relative, the finback, which is the second largest species, ranging in length from 60 to 80 feet. The humpback whale has never been very abundant, but along with the rorqual, or Sei Whale, it has provided an extra dividend for the business.

The extreme richness of the antarctic whaling grounds is due to the circumstance that the entire perimeter of the continent is open to oceanic waters, allowing whales free access to a tremendous area of fertile waters. On the other hand the limited richness of the arctic whaling grounds is attributable to the fact that the Arctic icecap is flanked principally by the land masses of Eurasia and North America so that the whales have had access only to those portions opening from the Bering Sea and to a small area in the North Atlantic. Whales cannot swim far in along the coast of either mainland because the period of open water is brief. Even in the antarctic whales tend to work near the ice floes and occasionally get caught by the sudden closures of the ice.

It is too difficult to estimate the number of whales which were taken from the arctic during the many seasons that whalers worked there. However, it cannot compare with the numbers which have been realized annually from the slaughter around Antarctica. As many as 45,000 whales have been taken in a brief whaling season of less than 2 months. Contracting governments under provision of the International Agreement For Regulation of Whaling enforce the regulations as regards the number taken and there is a penalty if a juvenile whale is killed. Nursing mothers are also protected. The regulations are made by the International Whaling Commission and the number of whales that can be taken each year is determined from the statistics of the populations. It is hoped that by these regulations and studies, the industry can continue to prosper. The problems and activities of the scientists, the majority of whom work for the various governments' agencies, will be considered shortly.

EARLY UNREGULATED WHALING
California Gray Whale

No account of whaling would be complete without mention of the shore and lagoon whaling of the California gray whale. Eleven shore whaling stations were scattered along the coast of California from San Simeon to San Diego, which had two stations. This whaling dates back to the gold rush days of California. It was not an uncommon experience for a whaling ship to come from the east and then to lose the entire crew in San Francisco before they could get on into the North Pacific to whale.

Although the principal profit for these whalers came from the arctic bowhead it was customary to return to San Francisco to resupply in the autumn, and then to whale the California gray during the winter migration.

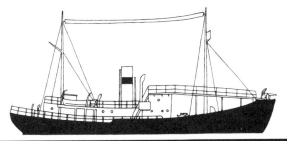

The two hump-back whales seen here at the Trinidad, California shore station were towed ashore for processing. Shore stations were practical when whales were abundant in coastal waters. As populations became depleted and prices for whale products diminished, shore stations were abandoned. Whaling was then carried on by large, efficient factory ships which could follow the whales throughout the oceans of the world.

49

Of course, this was whaling made to order because there was no need to search. The shore stations were able to process more whales in a day than a vessel could kill in a month of routine searching. Captain Scammon followed the migrating whales to the lagoons in Baja California where he found them calving. These lagoons became the headquarters for the whaling ships which found whaling even easier than they had along the migration route. One of these lagoons, Laguna Ojo de Liebre in Baja California, is known to English-speaking people as Scammon's Lagoon.

It was possible to watch the killing of whales from Point Loma, and from this vantage point the whaling boats were directed by flag signals to their quarry. The whales, once killed, were towed, tide permitting, by the hard rowing of the whaling crews back to Ballast Point. The numerous California shore stations have long since closed and rotted away and the grounds occupied with new enterprises. Most of the details of this era are lost forever or buried in yellowing manuscripts and newspapers.

Although the gray whale may have been easy to find and to approach, whalers noted that those which escaped had learned the implications of whaling and thereafter were difficult to take. Lagoon whaling was particularly hazardous because the mothers frequently would charge the boats. Much of the time of the ship's carpenter was used repairing the damaged boats. Of course, the exposure of the breeding and calving grounds to whaling had a catastrophic effect, for the whales soon disappeared. It is decidedly difficult to determine from the limited records which remain just how abundant the gray whale was before whaling started. One is likewise puzzled by the report that a thousand a day passed San Diego. If this estimate had been made by an experienced whaler it might be reliable, but if it were made by a layman it could be most inaccurate. It is doubtful that anyone would have actually counted the whales for even an hour, so that the figure is probably an exaggeration.

The decline in the abundance of the gray whale occurred during the period when whaling was nearly over because of the low price of oil. Two brief subsequent attempts to whale this species produced only a small return of individuals, leaving the species seemingly commercially extinct.

GRAY WHALE PROTECTED

In 1937 the International Whaling Commission declared the gray whale a protected species and forbade its members from whaling. The gray whale has recovered completely. There are estimated to be somewhere between 8,000 and 13,000 if the population has stabilized. Rice and Wolman, who have conducted both census and population dynamics from their sample of 316 whales, consider 1967 to be the year the population leveled off. They found that 44% of the sample were immatures, that is under eight years of age. The birth rate is 0.13% and the death rate must equal birth rate to achieve zero population growth. This mortality is made up largely of baby whales dead at birth or in the first weeks. Yearling whales make up the rest of observed mortality. If the gray whale lives to be 50 years old (and there is no reason to doubt that because the gray whale is not fully grown until the age 44) very few are dying from old age.

The International Whaling Commission at its annual meeting in 1978, accepted evidence that the California gray whale population had returned to a reasonable number and therefore the gray whale should be removed from the endangered list. It was decided that the Russian whaling fleets be permitted to harvest 300 gray whales to provide sustenance for their Siberian Eskimos.

VALUE OF GRAY WHALE

Esthetic

The whale has been viewed by hundreds of thousands of Californians and out of state visitors who have been thrilled to see such an animal. Currently each season excursion boats are transporting visitors on 2-hour excursions out to within a few hundred feet of the whales. Sportfishing vessels offer 4 and 6 day cruises to the calving grounds south of Scammon's Lagoon, which has been happily set aside as a sanctuary for the whales. Whale watching at Scammon's is now restricted to a whale overlook patterned after one at Cabrillo National Monument. These voyages also visit the offshore islands, where the whales tarry. Excursion boats operate along the migratory route from British Columbia south to San Diego. Over 135,000 school children from Los Angeles viewed the whales, and their experience was supervised by docents from the American Cetological Society. A strong effort to save whales for future generations is being made by all the conservation groups. It is hoped that the pleasure and education gained will transcend the brief monetary profit which might accrue to a few whalers. These and all life forms are unique and are therefore worthy of preservation for their own sake. It can be argued that even from an economic standpoint, the tourist and excursion operations transcend the gain that might come from the harvesting of this species. The continued decline in the number of whales and the concurrent reduction in the number of whaling companies has spurred conservationists into renewed efforts to push for complete cessation of whaling. There has been a proliferation of organizations devoting their efforts to this proposition on the grounds that whaling is morally degrading, unjust, and unnecessary because all the materials derived from the whale can be obtained from modern agricultural and chemical wizardry. Recently *The Wall Street Journal* reviewed the decline of whaling and pointed out that the loss of revenue from whaling has been more than offset by tourism which has sprung up along the Pacific Coast as people come out to watch the California gray whale. As humpback whales return in ever increasing numbers watching of these whales is contributing to the increase in tourism in Hawaii, Alaska, and Bermuda. Whale watching at sea is catching on along the coast of New England and into the Gulf of St. Lawrence, and extending up to Nova Scotia.

Scientific

There is real need to protect the gray whale for scientific studies. The principal problem in the study of populations of whales is to learn how large the population is and what forces limit its size. Such knowledge would make it possible for the industry to decide how many whales could be taken each season without reducing the population. The concept of taking only those whales which would overpopulate the habitat is an attractive one, since this would stabilize both the whale population and the industry.

Until now, the studies made to gain this knowledge have had to be made on populations that are under severe exploitation. The researcher can never be certain that his findings are normal and useful in estimating the total population. The California gray whale provides him with a controlled population that is not under predation by man. Furthermore, this population becomes concentrated during breeding and calving and briefly during migration so that counting the total population is feasible.

Commercial

There is the possibility that the whaling industry will resume the harvest of the California gray whale once the population has adequately recovered. This is indeed unfortunate as the species is not sufficiently abundant to provide much profit. Certainly history will repeat itself and the grand spectacle of the California gray whale migration will require another thirty or more years to repeat itself. The future status of the California gray whale may not necessarily have the same fortunate outcome, as the whaling industry at the present time is much more thorough. Furthermore, competition between the various whaling nations makes adjustment of regulations slow and cumbersome—much too slow for a species so limited in numbers and so liable to nearly complete extermination.

Already the Russians have expressed proprietary interest because they control the summer feeding grounds. Likewise, or by the same reasoning, the Mexicans control the breeding waters. The species would serve only as a supplementary one in areas where whaling is already marginal, because of limited stocks of commercial species. It is hoped that eventually the

 whaling interests will totally cease whaling for the gray whale leaving it as a living memorial to whaling.

NATURAL POPULATION CONTROLS

Conservationists should remember that nature has wisely designed each species of plant and animal with a built-in margin of safety; namely, a surplus of young which will repopulate the species after periods of extreme adversity. Yet these surpluses must somehow usually be eliminated, lest the species overpopulate its habitat and destroy its own sustenance. The controls that limit the population are many, and the population existing from year to year is the statistical average of these many controls. Diseases, predators, and other adversities are necessary evils, which are in the final analysis blessings in disguise. Whales, too, have their checks, although we are a long way from knowing their relative importance.

Perhaps the most critical moment in the life of the whale is birth, because the newborn whale must surface immediately or suffocate. Any abnormality in the birth process or weakness on the part of the infant may cause its loss. Inasmuch as a whale calves only every other year, the loss of a baby is serious, and especially so because a whale produces but a single calf. Less than one percent of whale births are twins (about the same frequency as for humans). A careful examination of the shores around the breeding lagoons reveals that a few babies are lost at birth. Balcomb recently described the birth. The female thrashes wildly upside down, and in labor both head and tail emerge from the water. The genital area is in the air and the baby suddenly emerges head first. The mother rolls over and supports the baby on her head until the breathing is not hurried. The afterbirth was not noted, and it has only been collected once despite the fact that in recent years hardly a day goes by that there isn't a qualified observer from the scientific community in one of the lagoons.

For a few days the baby's behavior suggest swimming with difficulty, with much spitting and sputtering. The baby swims poorly because its tail flukes are not well controlled, and swing out of the water on the upstroke. If frightened it begins to roll. Mother will quickly approach the floundering infant and move away with it on either her head or flipper. It is amazing to see how quickly the baby recovers its composure.

After a few days the baby may leave its mother to investigate a boat. Should this happen the mother may charge between baby and boat, showering occupants with a tremendous swing of her tail.

Now and then a mother will give birth en route to the lagoon. Although the mother in labor is conspicuous enough, once the baby is free she will travel slightly submerged with the baby swimming surfaced just above the tail. The baby doesn't dive deeply and exhales a small vapor-free spout once a minute. Mother with new born baby travels close into shore just beyond the surf or kelp. Cousteau reports that mothers on the northward migration are overlooked because of a similar route selection. He reports that the mother sends the baby into the kelp and will leave to return later. It has also been noted that in a lagoon a mother may leave her baby on a shoal area, clear of the tidal flow, and later return. No accounting of the baby-mother bond would be complete without noting the occasional occurrence of one or two orphans or abandoned babies.

CURRENT SCIENTIFIC INQUIRY

Life Expectancy

Life expectancy is another very useful statistic for population studies. The whaling industry has no easy way of determining this because whaling never gives an individual whale the chance to attain old age. Perhaps we can eventually determine life expectancy for the gray whale if the species remains protected from whaling. A further study would be necessary to determine what percentage of the population could be diverted to a renewed whaling industry.

Age Determination

The problem of aging whales is an important one, and one to which much thought has been given. Actually, it is desirable to know at what age sexual maturity occurs; at what age physical maturity; at what age reproduction is no longer possible, and lastly, the age at natural death. In addition, we need to know the gestation period and the average number of pregnancies of which the female is capable. Many of these statistics can be obtained from the examination of a freshly killed whale. Such age determinations are made on every specimen that comes aboard the factory ships, and also at the shore stations, but there is some doubt as to the accuracy of some determinations. Physical maturity is delayed in whales for many years, and it is judged complete when the cartilaginous end plates fuse to each vertebra (back-bone). After fusion, further lineal growth is impossible; after this time, whales have been noted to shrink slightly each year.

The other structures that a biologist collects for aging are the ovaries of the female whale. These are sliced across into half-inch slabs, and the number of exposed grayish masses are counted. One of these structures is produced for each pregnancy, and they persist as scar tissue throughout the life of the whale. These structures are functional during pregnancy and nursing and are responsible for a successful pregnancy. A count of these gives the investigator the total number of offspring that have been produced. If one assumes that the whale has not missed an opportunity to produce a baby, the count gives the age, assuming one knows the age at sexual maturity and the maximum length of bearing.

In recent years other indicators have been investigated so that the age of whales might also be determined. The best indicator is the cylinder of wax that fills the outer canal of the ear leading to the eardrum. This enlarges as the whale grows, and the growth is marked by banding very similar in appearance to tree rings. Slicing the plug, the rings can be exposed and counted. There are produced but two rings a year. Toothed whales can be aged by sawing teeth in half and noting the banding. Baleen also grows periodically, but this is more difficult to check because of wear.

Distribution and Population Rise

The whaling industry spends a few weeks before the whaling season and at the end, hunting whales with a much lighter gun, which implants a numbered cylinder deep in the skin of the whale. Each whale marked is logged as to the species, the latitude and longitude, and the date. Should the marked whale be processed in any succeeding season, a second entry is completed giving the date and place of capture. These records are used to determine the migration routes and the degree of intermingling of adjacent populations. The ratio of marked whales to unmarked whales allows the estimation of the probable size of the whale population. The length of time elapsing until a marked whale is recovered is an indication of the intensity of whaling.

In the fishing industry the reproductive potential of the fish is more than adequate to repopulate quickly, but in the whaling industry the reproductive potential is low. Only one-fourth of the population can contribute replacements each year, and then only a single baby. Of course, each offspring has a reasonable chance of reaching maturity, whereas very few fish achieve maturity.

One might expect that whales would be less affected by the fluctuations in environmental conditions, but this is only a surmise. We do not know as yet how to ascertain whether the food of whales is ever inadequate. Certainly the fact that baleen whales do best around the polar seas suggests that climatic fluctuations of the magnitude and duration of those producing ice ages may have profound effects on them.

If commercial whaling is to be continued, we can only hope that many will learn to exploit whales in such a way as to take only the surplus thereby creating a perpetual resource. Man can best profit aesthetically, scientifically and commercially by protecting the gray whale from whaling.

It appears unlikely that the magnificent whales now reduced to one tenth their original numbers can withstand the tremendous yearly loss in numbers (35,000) much longer. The whaling fleets of the Russian and Japanese exist because of their claimed need for food and raw biological materials. They have maintained their opposition to the wishes of the other nations who are willing to have a ten-year moratorium. It is hoped that man may soon develop a new awareness of these mammoths of the deep that will bring a complete end to their exploitation forever.

APPENDIX

Scientific names of all North American cetaceans with common names most in use. Maximum size indicated. Region: (A) Atlantic Ocean, (P) Pacific Ocean, (C) Circumpolar.

Scientific Name	Common Name	Size	Region
Order Cetacea	Whales, Dolphins, and Porpoises		
Suborder Odontoceti	Toothed Whales		
Family Ziphiidae	Beaked Whales		
Genus Berardius			
Berardius bairdii	Baird's Beaked Whale	42 ft.	(P)
Genus Mesoplodon			
Mesoplodon bidens	North Sea Beaked Whale	16 ft.	(A)
Mesoplodon densirostris	Dense-Beaked Whale	15 ft.	(A)
Mesoplodon europaeus	Antillean Beaked Whale	16 ft.	(A)
Mesoplodon mirus	True Beaked Whale	17 ft.	(A)
Mesoplodon stejnegeri	Bering Sea Beaked Whale	20 ft.	(P)
Mesoplodon carlhubbsi	Arch-Beaked Whale		(P)
Mesoplodon ginlegodens	Vernacular name?		(P)
Genus Ziphius			
Ziphius cavirostris	Cuvier's Beaked Whale	28 ft.	(A-P)
Genus Hyperoodon			
Hyperoodon ampullatus	Atlantic Bottlenosed Whale	30 ft.	(A)
Family Physeteridae	Sperm Whales		
Genus Physeter			
Physeter catodon	Sperm Whale	60 ft.	(A-P)
Family Kogiidae	Pigmy Sperm Whales		
Genus Kogia			
Kogia breviceps	Pigmy Sperm Whale	13 ft.	(A-P)
Kogia simus	Dwarf Sperm Whale	9 ft.	(A-P)
Family Monodontidae	White Whale and Narwhal		
Genus Delphinapterus			
Delphinapterus leucas	White Whale (Beluga)	18 ft.	(C)
Genus Monodon			
Monodon monoceros	Narwhal	12 ft.	(C)
Family Delphinidae	Dolphins and Porpoises		
Genus Stenella			
Stenella attenuata*	Slender-beaked Porpoise	6 ft.	(P)
Stenella frontalis*	Cuvier's Porpoise	6 ft.	(A)
Stenella graffmani*	Graffman's Porpoise	8 ft.	(P)
Stenella plagiodon*	Spotted Porpoise	7 ft.	(P)
Stenella longirostris	Long-snouted Porpoise	7 ft.	(A)
Family Delphinidae	Dolphins and Porpoises		
Genus Stenella			
Stenella caeruleoalba	Striped Dolphin	8 ft.	(A-P)
Genus Steno			
Steno bredanensis	Rough-toothed Porpoise	8 ft.	(A-P)

*All these supposed species (so marked) are regarded by Rice and Scheffer as synonyms or races of *Stenella dubia*. The species distinctions in *Delphinus* and *Tursiops* are also in doubt.

Scientific Name	Common Name	Size	Region
Genus Delphinus			
Delphinus delphis	Atlantic Dolphin	8 ft.	(A)
Delphinus bairdii	Pacific Dolphin	7 ft.	(P)
Genus Tursiops			
Tursiops truncatus	Atlantic Bottle-nosed Dolphin	12 ft.	(A)
Tursiops gilii	Gill's Bottle-nosed Dolphin	12 ft.	(P)
Tursiops nuuanu	Pacific Bottle-nosed Dolphin	7 ft.	(P)
Genus Lissodelphis			
Lissodelphis borealis	Right-whale Dolphin	8 ft.	(P)
Genus Lagenorhynchus			
Lagenorhynchus albirostris	White-beaked Dolphin	10 ft.	(A)
Lagenorhynchus acutus	Atlantic White-sided Dolphin	9 ft.	(A)
Lagenorhynchus obliquidens	Pacific White-sided Dolphin	7 ft.	(P)
Lagenorhynchus thicolea	Gray's White-sided Dolphin	9 ft.	(P)
Genus Orcinus			
Grampus orca	Atlantic Killer Whale	30 ft.	(A)
Grampus rectipinna	Pacific Killer Whale	30 ft.	(P)
Genus Grampus			
Grampus griseus	Grampus or Risso's Dolphin	13 ft.	(A-P)
Genus Pseudorca			
Pseudorca crassidens	False Killer Whale	18 ft.	(A-P)
Genus Globicephala			
Globicephala melaena	Common Blackfish or (Pilot Whale)	28 ft.	(A)
Globicephala macrorhyncha	Short-finned Blackfish	20 ft.	(A)
Globicephala scammonii	Pacific Blackfish	16 ft.	(P)
Genus Feresa			
Feresa attenuata	Pygmy Killer Whale	8 ft.	(P)
Genus Phocoena			
Phocoena phocoena	Harbor Porpoise	6 ft.	(A)
Phocoena sinus	Gulf of California Porpoise	5 ft.	(P)
Genus Phocoenoides			
Phocoenoides dalli	Dall's Porpoise	7 ft.	(P)
Suborder Mysticeti	Baleen Whales		
Family Eschrichtiidae	Gray Whale		
Genus Escrichtius			
Eschrichtius gibbosus	California Gray Whale	50 ft.	(P)
Family Balaenopteridae	Rorqual Whales		
Genus Balaenoptera			
Balaenoptera physalus	Fin-back or Fin Whale or Fin-back Whale	81 ft.	(A-P)
Balaenoptera borealis	Sei Whale	60 ft.	(A-P)
Balaenoptera edeni	Bryde's Whale		(A-P)
Balaenoptera acutorostrata	Little Piked or Minke Whale	33 ft.	(A-P)
Balaenoptera musculus	Blue (Sulphur-bottom) Whale	100 ft.	(A-P)
Genus Megaptera			
Megaptera novaeangliae	Hump-backed Whale	50 ft.	(A-P)
Family Balaenidae	Right and Bowhead Whales		
Genus Balaena			
Eubalaena glacialis	Atlantic Right Whale	70 ft.	(A-P)
Balaena mysticetus	Bowhead Whale	65 ft.	(C)

BIBILIOGRAPHY

ALPENS, A. 1961. Dolphins, the Myth and the Animal. Houghton Mifflin. 268 p.

AUDUBON Magazine, January, 1975. (Special Whale issue)

ANDERSON, H.T. The Biology of Marine Animals. Acad. Press N.Y. 511 p.

ANDREWS, R.C., 1914. Monographs of the Pacific Cetacea I. The Calif. Gray whale. Rachianectes glaucus. Mem. Amer. Mus. Nat. Hist. N.S. 1 (5): 229-87.

BALCOMB, K.C. 1974. The Birth of a Gray Whale. Pac. Discovery 27 (3):28-31.

BEDDARD, F.E. 1900. A book of Whales. G.P. Putman and Sons IV. 320 p.

BRANDT, K. 1940 Whale Oil—Economic Analysis. Food Res. Inst. Stanford Univ. Fats and Oil Studies. #7:241 p.

COUSTEAU, JACQUE— Yves and P. Diole. 1972. The Whale Mighty Monarch of the Sea. Doubleday and Co. Inc. Garden City, N.Y. 1 -304

CUMMINGS, W.C., P.O. Thompson and R. Cook. 1968. Underwater Sounds of Migrating Gray Whales. Eschritius glaucus (cope). J. Acoustic Res. 44:1278-81

DAUGHERTY, A.E., 1965. Marine Mammals of Calif. Dept. Fish Game. 87 p.

FISH, JAMES F., J.L. Sumich and G.L. Lingle. 1974. Sound produced by the Gray Whale. Eschritius robustus. Marine Fisheries Review 36(4): 38-45

GASKIN, D.E. 1972. Whales, Dolphins and Seals. With special preference to the New Zealand area. St. Martin Press. 1-200.

GILMORE, R.M. 1961. The Story of the Gray Whale. Author priv. pub. 1-17.

HARE, LLOYD. 1960. Salted Tories, Marine Hist. Assoc. Mystic.

HARRISON, R.J. and J.E. King. Marine Mammals. Hutchinson Univ. Lib. 192 p.

HENDERSON, D.A. 1970. Journal aboard the Bark Ocean Bird on a Whaling Voyage at Scammon's Lagoon. Winter of 1858-1859. By Charles Melville Scammon. Dawson's Book Store, Los Angeles, 78 p.

HENDERSON, D.A. 1972. Men and Whales of Scammon's Lagoon. Dawson's Book Store, Los Angeles. 1-303.

HESKKOVITZ, P. 1966. Catalogue of Living Whales. Bull US. Nat. Mus. 246: 1-259.

HOLLAND, F. and T. Walker. 1964. Nineteenth Century Shore Whaling in San Diego, The Western Explorer. Vol 3(2):13-19.

HOWELL, A.B. 1930. Aquatic Mammals. Their Adaptations to Life in Water. C.C. Thomas Springfield.

JENKINS, J.T. 1921. A history of the whale fishery from the Basque fisheries of the 10th century to the finner whales at the present date. 336 p.

JENKINS, J.T. 1948. Bibliography of Whaling. J. Soc. Bibliography Nat. Hist. 2:71-166.

KELLOGG, R. 1940. Whales, Giants of the Sea. Nat. Geogr. 77:35-90.

KELLOGG, W.N. 1961. Porpoises and Sonar. U. of Chicago Press.

LEATHERWOOD, S.W.E. Evans and D.W. Rice. 1972. The whales, dolphins and porpoises of the Eastern North Pacific: a guide to their identification in the water. Naval Undersea Center, San Diego. 1-174 p.

MARINE Fisheries Review Vol. 36 Number 4 April 1974 (Special Gigi issue)

MATTHEWS, L.H. 1968. The Whale. London, 1968. 287 p.

MELVILLE, H. 1946. Moby Dick or the Whale. Cresset Press. London.

NORMAN, J.R. and F.C. Fraser. 1948. Giant Fishes, Whales and Dolphins. Putman, Lond.

NAYMAN, J. 1973. Whales, Dolphins and Man. Hamlyn. 1-28.

NORRIS, K.S. (Ed.). Whales, porpoises and dolphins. H. of C. Berk. 789 p.

ORR, R.T. Animals in Migration. MacMillan. 1-303.

ORR, R.T. 1972. Marine Mammals of Calif. Calif. Nat. Hist. Guide #29. U. of Calif. Press. 1-64.

PEDERSEN, T. and J.T. Rand. 1946. Bibliography of Whales and Whaling. Hvalradets Skrifter. #30.

PIKE, G.C. 1962. Migration and Feeding of the Gray Whale. *Eschritius gibbosus*. J. Fish. Res. Bd. Canada. 19(5): 815-838.

RICE, DALE W. and Victor B. Schaefer. 1968. A list of the marine mammals of the world. U.S. Fish and Wildlife Service Special Scientific Report—Fisheries No. 579. 16 p.

RICE, DALE W. and A.A. Wohlman. 1971. The life history and ecology of the gray whale. *Eschritius robustus*. Am. Soc. Mammal. Special Publ. #3. 142 p.

RIDGEWAY, SAM H., Editor 1972. Mammals of the Sea; Biology and Medicine. Charles C. Thomas, Springfield, Illinois. 812 p.

RIEDMAN, SARAH R. and E. T. Gustafson. 1966. Home is the Sea: for Whales.

SANDERSON, I.T., 1956. Follow the Whale. Little, Brown and Co. Boston.

SCAMMON, C.M. 1874. The Marine Mammals of the Northwestern Coast of North America. John W. Carmany and Co. San Francisco. 319 p.

SCHEELE, W.E. The First Mammals. World Publishing. Clev. N.Y.

SCHEFFER, V. 1969. Year of the Whale. Scribner, N.Y. 1-214.

SCHEFFER, VICTOR B. and J.W. Sokpp. 1948. The whales and dolphins of Wash. State with a key to the cetaceans of the west coast of North America. Am. Midl. Nat. 39: 257-337.

SHEPARD, F.B. and H.R. Wainless. 1971. Our Changing Coastlines. McGraw Hill. 1-579 p.

SLIFPER, E.J. 1962. Whales. Basic Books Inc. 1962. 475 p.

SLIJPER, E.J. 1936. Capila Zool. 7 (1-500). Comp. Anatomy Whales.

SMALL, G. 1971. Blue Whale. Columbia Univ. Press. 248 p.

SQUIRE, Ina L. 1964. A bibliography of Cetacea. Literature published between 1949 and 1963. Clearinghouse for Federal scientific and technical information. U. S. Naval Ord. Ted. Station unclassified ADG13005. 1-114.

STARBUCK, 1878. History of American Whale Fishery from its earliest inception to the year 1976. Weltham, Mass. 1-768.

SUND, P. 1975. Evidence of feeding during migration of an early birth of the Calif. Gray Whale. *(Eschritius robustus)* Jour. Mom. 56(1): 265-66.

TOMILIN, A.G. 1967. Mammals of USSR and adjacent countries. Jerusblen Prog. Sci. Travel Pl. 9 717 p.

VAN DEINSE, A.B. and G.C.A. Junge. 1937. Recent and older finds of the Calif. Gray Whale in the Atlantic. Temminckia. 2:161-88.

WALKER, T.J. 1969. Detection of Marine Organisms by an Infrared Mapper. Woods Hole Symposium on Oceanography from Space. p. 321-35.

WALKER, T.J. 1971. The Calif. Gray Comes Back. Nat. Geog. 1971, March. 394-415.

WILLIAMS, E. One Whaling Family. Houghton Mifflin.

YOUNG, J.Z. The life of Mammals. Oxford Univ. Press. 820 p.